The Whisper of Dreams
A Collection of Poetry

Editors
Rebecca S. Bell
C. Sherman Severin

Illustrator
Mindy Miller

Introduction by
Curt L. Sytsma

CSS Publications
Post Office Box 23
Iowa Falls, Iowa 501126

Copyright 1982 by C. Sherman Severin & Rebecca S. Bell
CSS Publications, P.O. Box 23, Iowa Falls, Iowa 50126

All rights reserved

Library of Congress Catalog Number:
ISBN: 0-942170-04-0

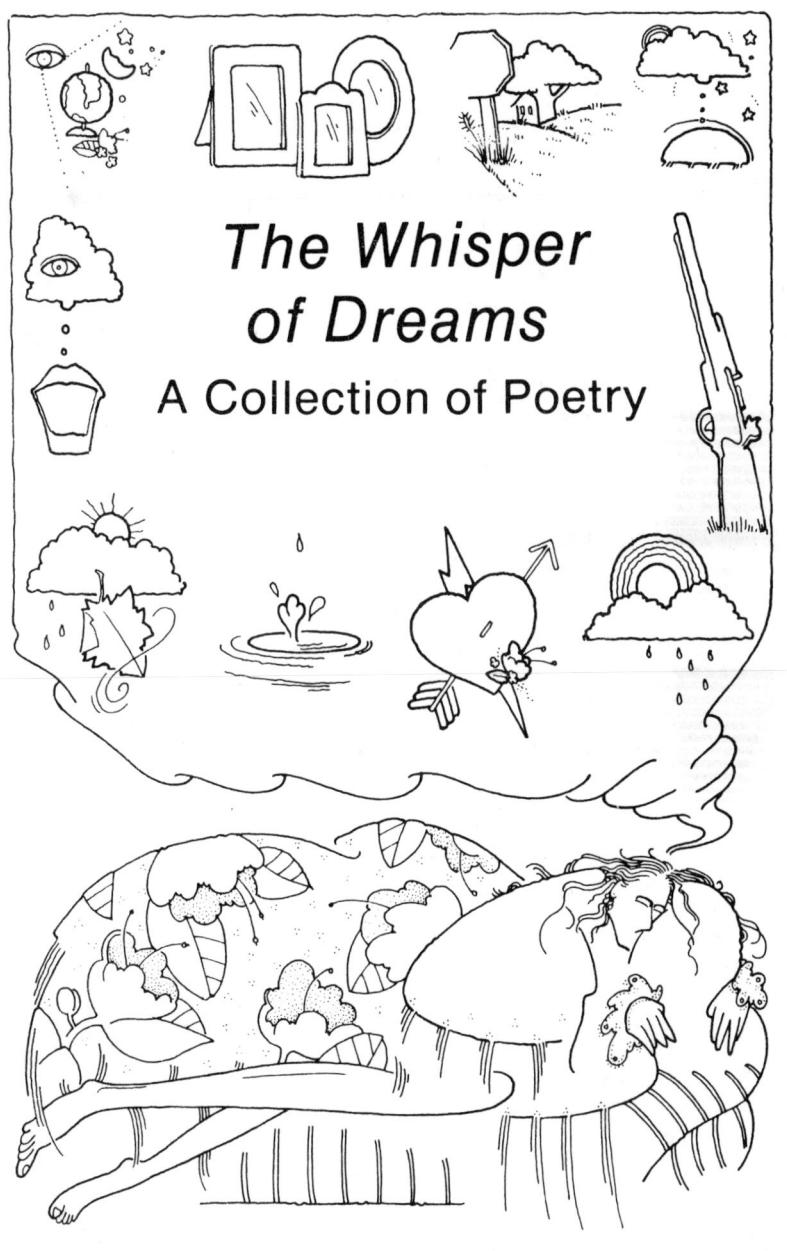

The Whisper of Dreams
A Collection of Poetry

*This Book is Dedicated
to Sherman & Our Shared Dream*

Credits

Publisher: CSS Publications
Iowa Falls, Iowa

Editors: Rebecca S. Bell
C. Sherman Severin

Illustrator: Mindy Miller

Design: Rebecca S. Bell

Typesetters: M.S. Page
Paul Beck

Special Thanks: Gladys Bell
Mike Bell
Margie Smith
Curt L. Sytsma
Robert C. Gremmels

About the Book

The Whisper of Dreams resulted from the fifth annual poetry contest sponsored by CSS Publications in 1982. The contest, based on the theme of "human emotions," officially ended on March 15.

All entries were read by an 11-member panel of judges (listed in the last chapter of this book), and they selected the poems which appear in this book. They determined which poems were the prize-winning poems and nominated those designated with an honorable mention.

The book was designed and produced by Editor Rebecca Bell in a process that took the entire summer. She was meticulous and careful in the composition of the chapters, integrating themes and ideas so as to emphasize the meaning and importance of each individual poem.

The Whisper of Dreams is divided into 10 chapters. Biographical sketches of all poets included in the section appear immediately following the chapter title page.

For the first time in this series of poetry anthologies, poems by members of the panel of judges are included in the book. They appear in the final chapter, "Interpreters (What the Dream is Saying)."

The Whisper of Dreams beckons . . . .

Preface

A Little Magic

A dream shared by C. Sherman Severin and Rebecca S. Bell was the inspiration on which CSS Publications was founded in 1977. The dream has been merely a whisper in our minds, prompting us to sponsor annual poetry contests and then produce an anthology from the best entries.

The full realization of that dream, however, did not come until the publication of this book, *The Whisper of Dreams*. And, even when the book was in production, we did not know that this one would epitomize the dream....

But the magic of each preceding volume of poetry, and the magic of meeting poets at our annual banquets, and the magic of being involved with the judges and the printers and the office staff... has culminated in the realization of that dream. This book fully captures the essence of the dream whispered to us more than five years ago.

There's a magic in poetry. It is, indeed, the whisper of dreams spoken softly to individuals receptive enough to hear . . . and talented enough to be able to articulate them through the vehicle of a poem.

There's magic in *The Whisper of Dreams*. The book contains the combined magic of the individual voices speaking in a whisper; the chapters amplify those softly spoken messages coming from inner worlds into an audible voice.

If you listen closely, the magic of these whispered dreams will mesmerize you, too....

Introduction

Daring to Dream

In writing the introduction to this fifth annual anthology of verse by CSS Publications, a single question haunts me with an almost brutal relevance: What dare I dream?

Dare I dream that this volume will introduce tomorrow's Walt Whitman to the world? Dare I hope that a twentieth century Alexander Pope is waiting within, shortly to be discovered, or that a modern Emily Dickinson is shyly peering from its pages, yearning for recognition? Should I pretend to an omnipotent competence and praise this book with imitations of immortality?

I think not.

Such dreams are fine, but, somehow, they are less worthy than the reality. The reality is an anthology of a people's soul, and the poems in this book are like us all — human, uncertain and hopeful, whispering dreams against the winds of change.

In politics, in America, there are forums aplenty for the expression of the people's views. There is the voting box, the polls, the letters to the editors, the public hearings. There are demonstrations and parades and soap-boxes. We can be heard — and heard loudly —on everything from taxes to foreign policy.

There are not, however, so many forums available for the expression of the people's *emotions*. The poetic whispers are lost in the shouts of protest, and the loss is a grievous one. There is a needed solace in the intimate parings of our neighbor's soul that no political forum can replace.

This book is a forum for the people's emotions, and, in its pages, you will find a shared comfort for your private pains and a shared ecstacy for your private joys. You will see the visions that came quietly, one by one, to poets across the country. You will hear the wonder of the whispered word.

Dylan Thomas said that the world is never the same once a good poem has been added to it. He was right, and the reason is as basic as humanity itself. There is a core of emotional truth in every soul, and the baring and sharing of that core is poetry. In this respect, every poem in this book is a masterpiece and every author appearing on its pages is a genius.

And, if perchance, a Walt Whitman *is* waiting to be discovered within, well . . . it doesn't hurt to dream.

Curt L. Sytsma
Des Moines, Iowa
August, 1982

Contents

SPECTRUM

3	Spectrum/*Marlana Coe*
4	Banana, Orange & Kiwi Fruit/*CSS Poets*
5	The Lion/*Martha K. Graham*
6	The Northeast Corner/*Vernor Rodgers, III*
7	6/27/78 and Popes Still Die/*Lance Covert*
8	Jonah Revisited/*Teresa Burleson*
9	Despair/*Mary Rauch*
10	Loneliness/*James Frazer*
11	Loneliness Within/*Tapendu K. Basu*
11	The Shadow/*Vernelia B. Jobe*
12	The Worst/*Jon Bush*
12	Disappointments/*Sally Hull Wiebe*
13	Oft' Times/*Paul Lee Thomas, II*
13	Hopelessness/*Tammy Lyman*
14	The Book is Ours/*Pauline Grey*
14	Knowledge/*Deborah J. Clark*
15	Inspiration/*Esther Edleman*
15	This Poet's Prayer/*Karen E. Thomas*
16	For Emily Dickinson/*Darrell H. Bartee*
17	Writing//*David R. Ross*
18	Pinesol/*Chema Ude*
19	Supermarketing in the 80's/*Cholm G. Houghton*
20	Contemplation/*J. Kay Lowe*
22	Budget Cuts/*Linda Black Curtis*

PORTRAITS
- 25 Portrait/*Martha K. Graham*
- 26 The Rapist/*Helen E. Rilling*
- 27 A Couple of Swingers/*Marsha A. Mitchell*
- 28 New Pupil/*Elaine D. Hardt*
- 29 The Clown Crier/*Ann Johnson*
- 29 Memory/*Kathleen Ela*
- 30 The Way Bill Is/*Noni Bookbinder Bell*
- 31 Jeanne/*Helen E. Rilling*
- 32 Bird Lady/*Marsha A. Mitchell*
- 33 Jessie/*Judy V. Keyser*
- 34 My Sombrero/*Roy Barlag*
- 36 Stephane's Song/*Robert A. Julius*
- 36 The Safecracker's Dream/*John L. Lozes*
- 38 Marianne/*Bob Summers*
- 38 The Gambler/*Carmie Peintner*

FROM THE CORNER
- 41 From the Corner/*Jean Kennedy*
- 42 The Midwest (in Five Parts)/*Lynne Proctor Sancken*
- 44 This Quiet Lane/*Joseph A. Sweet*
- 46 Skipping Stones/*John Sharsmith*
- 47 Cleaning Fish/*Glen Enloe*
- 48 Cathedral Chimes/*Janet Smith*
- 48 Help/*Dianna Randall*
- 49 Do You Believe?/*Max Maxon*
- 50 To An Old House/*Martha K. Graham*
- 51 Sun-Warmed Memory/*Tracy Grandy*
- 52 Gone/*Linda Black Curtis*
- 54 Foreclosure Sale/*Helen E. Rilling*
- 56 Requiem for a General Store/*Laurre Breman*
- 58 Reverie & Wails/*Doris T. Brokaw*

INTROSPECTION
- 61 Introspection/*Jean Marie Schultz*
- 62 Reflections of a Wall Flower/*Don Helmstetter*
- 62 Winter Poem, 1980/*Ann Lynn Smith*
- 63 Broken Glass/*J. Karyl Arnold*
- 64 Adrift/*Margaret Matthews Bradley*
- 65 Life from the Sea/*Peg Barry*

66	How Many Times/*R. J. Caylor*
68	Wide Awake Dreams/*Constance Leigh Rentel*
69	Dreams with a Shadowed Past/*Sue Ann Cardwell*
70	Umbrellas/*Bruce Stansberry*
71	Windhorse/*Michael G. Kelly*
72	Meditation/*Rebecca Lakanen*
73	Emotions in Retrospect/*Phylis Williams*
74	Unseen Dimensions/*Gurley Starlin*
75	The Shadow Stone/*Bill Forsythe*
76	The Face of Truth/*Nicholas Atkinson*
77	Hidden Truths/*Lydia Hartunian*
78	The Light Touch/*Alice Mackenzie Swaim*
79	Insomnia/*Esther Mennen*
80	Haiku/*Mildred Hope Wood*
80	Haiku/*Esther Edleman*

ARTILLERY

83	Artillery/Perimeter/Okinawa/*Arthur C. Frick*
84	Out of the Cradle/*Janet Madison*
85	The Head Nurse & the Warrior/*Melvin F. Stephens*
86	Interview with a Veteran, 1980/*Will C. Jumper*
87	Roosevelt's Birthday/*Jim Albright*
88	Taps/*Frances Conklin French*
89	First Shot/*Joseph H. Oates*
90	Middle West (in Protest of Nuclear War)/
90	*Glenda Winders*
91	Countdown/*Curt L. Sytsma*
94	Lessons Learned by Survivors/*Michael G. Kelly*

TOMORROW'S RAIN

97	Tomorrow's Rain/*Emily Rose*
97	Winter/*Gail Dane*
98	Victory/*Eartha Sarah Melzer*
98	Love/*Erika Thomas*
99	The Snowstorm in Me/*Tara Lynn Herringa*
99	One Track Mind/*Michael F. Felsburg*
100	Feelings in Flight/*Andrew Robert Schuhler*
100	Fog/*Jennifer Simpson*
101	My Hopes & Dreams/*Becki Witte*
102	Together (Friends)/*Angela Vyverberg*

LOVE DOES THAT

105	Love Does That/*Jane Griggs*	
105	Giggles in the Wind/*Cheryl Sanders*	
106	Dear Friend/*Margery Disburg*	
107	Upon Visiting an Old Friend/*Carol Fox Thorne*	
108	She & I/*E. Mellenia DeCoteau Jones*	
109	A Step Behind/*Ronald L. Andrzejewski*	
110	Waiting/*Glenda Winders*	
111	To a Marble Statue in a Public Park/*Eleanor M. Kerr*	
112	The Meeting/*Jill Hamilton*	
113	Take My Hand/*Kathie Jacquin*	
114	About Dawes Park/*Judy Keyser*	
115	See Through Snowfall/*Mila Gudding*	
116	Minor Revision/*Thom Ross*	
116	Waiting/*Glenda Winders*	
118	Sometimes: A Sestina/*Sheila Joy Packa*	
119	Sierra Dawn/*Carl E. Gillespie, Jr.*	
120	1, 2, U/*Mark Lawson*	
121	Smiling/*Sharon Harris*	
121	Dove/*Kathleen O'Brien Davin*	
122	Performing Bear/*J. Karyl Arnold*	
122	Friendship/*Mike Paul*	
123	Love Gone Awry/*Georgiann Hagen*	
124	Crushed Petals/*Nancy Brier O'Neal*	
125	Spring Thaw/*Doris Brokaw*	
126	Distances/*Eva S. Wood*	
127	Checkmate/*Tina Abolins*	
128	Rupture/*Pamela Snow*	
128	The Blades/*Rob Ross*	
129	Madness of No Method/*Brian Finney*	
130	Watercolor/*Brenda R. Johnson*	
131	Forbidden/*L. J. Szumylo*	
131	Casualty/*Mike Paul*	
132	Missing You/*Eva S. Wood*	
133	Leavetaking/*Martha K. Graham*	
134	Nightmoth/*Michael G. Kelly*	
135	Life/*Jane Terrando*	
136	Love's Resurrection/*Nola Deffenbaugh*	

CONCENTRIC CIRCLES

- 139 Concentric Circles/*William P. Riddle*
- 140 My House/*Nelle McCain*
- 141 In the Morning/*Kathy A. Olson*
- 142 Present with a Past/*De Anne Richtsmeier*
- 143 Cages/*Dorthy M. Ross*
- 144 Apples for the Oven/*Marilyn J. Barnes*
- 145 Cold Turkey/*Pat King*
- 146 Returned Embrace/*Constance Leigh Rentel*
- 147 Parting with a Missionary Daughter/ *Rosemary Freeman*
- 148 The Mother/*Enid M. Bennett*
- 149 Mother/*Lori Fitterling*
- 150 A Mother's Prayer/*Agnes K. Bogardus*
- 151 About Children/*Betty C. Moore*
- 152 A Treasure/*Sally C. Medernach*
- 152 Discovery/*Karen Murguia*
- 153 Branding/*Becky Foght Melby*
- 154 My Children Are Made of Me/*Judy White*
- 155 One/*Patricia L. Anderson*
- 155 Hero Worship/*Sandy Liska*
- 156 Answer/*Garrett W. Floyd*
- 157 Grandson/*Zelma Bomar*
- 157 Granddaughters/Grandsons/*Jeannette Garafola*
- 158 A Belated Apology/*LeRoy Heckman*
- 159 Missing/*Christine Christian*
- 160 Generation Gap/*Joan Merryman Burns*
- 162 The Lure/*Sue Anne Briggs*
- 163 The Pain/*Marilyn J. Barnes*
- 164 Elegy for a Marriage/*Melody Moody*
- 166 Marriage on the Rocks/*Constance Leigh Rentel*
- 166 Now That You Are Gone/*Constance Leigh Rentel*
- 168 I Never Used to Hear You/*Deloris Slesiensky*
- 169 Say Again/*Mary Dupont*
- 170 Change/*June L. Shipley*
- 171 That Man's Lobster/*Lauren McDowell-Kurszewski*
- 172 To N.F.J./*Evelyn J. Boettcher*
- 173 Many Things Fall/*Mary Lou Sanelli*
- 174 Prognostication (1)/*Dorothy Moore*
- 175 Prognostication (2)/*Dorothy Moore*
- 176 Going Home/*T. R. Felice*

SEASONED WITH S's

- 179 Seasoned with S's/*Patti A. Nemec*
- 180 April's Spring/*Sister Monica Lammers*
- 181 Early Summer/*Jean Marie Schultz*
- 182 Summer Comes Again/*Russell T. Runnels*
- 183 40th Street Summer/*Gary D. Moore*
- 184 Hidden Beauty/*Edna Dame*
- 185 Night/*Ralph Kudish*
- 186 Rainy Day/*Joy (Smith) Leister*
- 187 Absence of Rain/*J. Kay Lowe*
- 188 Autumn Mood/*Marianne Bern*
- 189 Leavings/*Jean Kennedy*
- 190 The Music of Autumn/*Dondeena Caldwell*
- 190 Alms Aims/*Grace Rasmussen*
- 191 October/*Saralyn M. Smith*
- 192 Watcher in the Mountains/*Darrell H. Bartee*
- 192 Haiku/*Esther Edleman*
- 193 November Song/*Ann Foley*
- 194 Sad Thoughts May Linger/*Doris M. Colter*
- 195 *Winter Storm Watch/Nancy Smith*
- 196 Cabin Fever/*Suzanne Kelsey*
- 197 Winter Night/*Martha K. Graham*
- 198 Winter's End/*Marilyn J. Romine Mattix*

INTERPRETERS (What The Dream Is Saying)

- 201 Thirty Billion Stars/*Phelps/Bruner*
- 201 For Those I Love/*Phelps/Bruner*
- 202 The Wait/*Charlotte H. Bruner, Translator*
- 203 Getting Next to Me/*Betty Hall*
- 203 Rites/*Betty Hall*
- 204 Born Losers/*Betty Hall*
- 205 Advice to a Collector/*Will C. Jumper*
- 205 Advice to a Builder/*Will C. Jumper*
- 206 Valentine/*Kathleen Peirce*
- 207 Fog/*Kathleen Peirce*
- 209 What the Dream is Saying/*Kathleen Peirce*
- 210 Charlie/*Sarah P. Simmons*
- 211 Conversation/*Sarah P. Simmons*
- 212 At the Potter's House/*Sarah P. Simmons*
- 214 The Day is June/*Curt L. Sytsma*

Spectrum

DARRELL H. BARTEE is a Hoosier, living at times in Colorado, New York and Kansas, now a widower. His poetry, articles, fiction and light verse have been published, to quote him, "all over."... **TAPENDU K. BASU,** a physician, would love to devote more time to writing; he hopes someday he will. His dream is "one world, one nation — with many colorful people."... **JON BUSH,** 25, has been writing for many years and has been published in "little" magazines and several anthologies. His other interests include fine arts and basketball.... **TERESA BURLESON,** a graduate from Texas A&M in journalism, has written for a newspaper, taught school, and is now putting her husband through seminary. "For me, poetry is an expression of the manifold grace of God, a way of glorifying Him. Without Him, there would be no poem.". ... **MARLANA COE,** 27, has a master's in French literature and now lives and writes in the Rocky Mountains of Montana.... **DEBORAH J. CLARK,** 23, is the wife of a cattleman and mother of 3. She gained an interest in writing poetry through her high school poetry classes. Outside of a high school publication, this is her first published poem.... **LANCE COVERT,** 25, loves to mow the lawn. He writes while standing on his head.... **LINDA BLACK CURTIS,** 46, is a political volunteer, a social worker and a union member. Poetry helps put it all together.... **ESTHER EDLEMAN** is proud to find her poems published in all 5 CSS Publications anthologies. For her, prose & poetry writing has always been a spontaneous creative outlet. "My verses help me to maintain a proper perspective in my life. I enjoy sharing them with kindred spirits."... **JAMES E. FRAZER,** 60, has been writing poetry for 40 years, but this is his first publication. He has been married for 37 years & has 8 children & 7 grandchildren. A veteran of World War II and Vietnam, he is recently retired from the Air Force. He enjoys camping, hiking, golf, swimming & writing.... **MARTHA K. GRAHAM,** a retired school teacher, is an active teacher of piano & organ. "I love teaching, reading, traveling, observing the natural world, writing poetry & prose, and spending all time possible at our 150-year old house, with its 7 acres of woods, on the Mississippi just north of Hamelton, Illinois."... **PAULINE GREY** is a life member of the Kansas Authors Club and has won many prizes in poetry and other categories in both state & district annual contests. Her work has appeared in a number of national publications.... **CHOLM G. HOUGHTON,** 69, retired in 1969 as vice president of Livestock Conservation Institute after a 45-year career in journalism. Youngest of a family of 8, he was graduated in 1934 from the University of Iowa; he is married and has 2 grown children & 2 grandchildren.... **VERNELIA PREBLE JOBE,** mother of 10 & grandmother of 30, enjoys photography, writing and gardening. She lives on a farm in rural Wisconsin with her husband, Walter, who raises feeder pigs.... **J. KAY LOWE,** 42, is a mother of 2 children and took an active part in raising 3 more children through a second marriage. She is employed as office manager at Camp Foster YMCA and enjoys jogging, gardening, quilting & night classes.... **TAMMY LYMAN,** 15, is a sophomore at Bolivar High. Writing poetry has always been a favorite pastime for her, along with reading and being active in sports.... **MARY RAUCH** says, "When I wrote 'Despair,' my husband was devoting all his time to his profession. Jesus heard me crying. He brought me up out of the valley into His sunshine, baptized us both with His Holy Spirit, and gave us 'A New Song.' We praise His Holy Name!".... **VERNOR RODGERS, III,** 27, is the sports editor of Foothill Inter-City Newspapers in Arcadia. He is a fan of cinema and has been writing poetry for 10 years. He is currently completing his first novel.... **DAVID R. ROSS,** 28, is a student at the University of Iowa. He writes mostly for small press publications and has no other plans at the moment.... **KAREN EMELIA THOMAS,** 20, has

Continued on page 40...

Spectrum

Sadness. Comes in musks
of trite blues, reeking of honky tonks
and one night stands.

Pensiveness. Not Rodin's great man
but a country parson
walking the church graveyard.
His greatest congregation lies there.

Hopelessness. An old hooker, wrinkled and hoarse.
Bloated, too much rouge . . .
Standing on the corner under a neon halo.

Melancholy. Pulls in gut notes
from a New Orleans saxophone. Wails
over plains and echoes through mountains,
reaching from the hottest pits of hell
to the firiest balls of heaven.

Grief. Bent back and bloodied hands:
a farmer watching hail beat down
his only crop of corn.

Anger. Psychologists' plaything. Animals'
instinct. Man's regret.

Happiness. A rainbow, complete
with a pot of gold foil wrapped chocolates.
A mixture of dew
and bird throated colors: a witch's tonic.

Joy. A baby discovers his foot. Columbus
discovered America. Apple pie
sometimes burns.

Marlana Coe
Helena, Montana

Banana, Orange and Kiwi Fruit

"Too many cooks may spoil a broth, but humanity has never known such a thing as too many poets.
— *the phantom philosopher*

I crept into myself.
The visual method of protection,
    smiles masking confusion,
    confusion masking smiles;
Coming apart . . .
Images shattered . . .
Wondering alone . . .
We moved the desk out to make room for the settee;
The door at the floor named 5 demanded a key.
A neighbor with insomnia cursed the noise.
    Rightly so.
        Isn't it nice to whisper?
        Enter laughing, gently.
        Enter jestors, softly.
        Enter silence
            in Sweet Surrender.
Cycles; crimes.
Animals; chimes.
Lavender is my bathroom color.
Purple channels;
Glass beds shudder;
Fortune's obese unflattering dimension;
    But,
        Isn't it nice to whisper?

*A Group Effort by Poets Attending
the Second Annual CSS Publications Poetry
Awards Banquet/Ames, Iowa/December 10, 1981.*

The Lion

I would not have come here
if I had remembered
how the lions pace
up and down
up and down
passing each other with no sign.

Today one stopped,
and there in the half light
I saw raw anguish burning.

Challenge flared,
flickered once
and died.

Shaken,
I turned away.

But on through the long labyrinth
echoing with screams and cries and mutterings,
the lion followed,
and still follows.

"Whose is this guilt?" I ask of the iron bars.

It is not the honest animal-stench of the place
I am sick with.

Outside at last,
I breathe in the clean, bright air.
But in the sky
the very sun's a lion's eye.

Martha K. Graham
Macomb , Illinois

Honorable Mention

The Northeast Corner

The El Dorado String Quartet
Massaged its instruments in dismay
A grimace tightened my soul
My knees buckled as I fell to pray

Self pity held my psyche hostage
Woe is me, I cried this apt cliche
But the Northeast Corner sizzled
Ten million brain cells held me at bay

Cerebral terrorism shined
The brass section spit out its segue
A relay team transporting tears
Was hijacked, tossed into the subway

The Northeast Corner emcee laughed
All latitudes line up, he would say
Only six percent of his mind
Seems willing to smirk without delay

Cat gut screamed and I became deaf
Nosedived into a porcelain tray
Sorrow planned retaliation
Greybeards anted up for the parlay

The outside world stood, hands on hips
The Northeast Corner named the play
An oil of giddiness washed up
I laughed, cried, bellowed and sighed all day

Dusk fell, the Northeast Corner heaved
A vibrating execution stay
A fragile peace strengthened my soul
It was groping blindly not to stray

Vernor Rodgers III
Arcadia, California

6/26/78 and Popes Still Die

    It's drizzling dusk
tittering dully on the alley eyed window
        Bitter Beauty wrapped in a torn sheet
      sitting on a cushioned chair
      diagrams her cynicism
        as I paint her toenails

    White wine
    Whispers
               and
prowling chicken soup mingles
    with her maritme aroma
        She clutches the linen about her tighter
      as
      Cool Gabriel
    with a horn mute
      blows
    drawn neon brass
        it slides down the gutted hallway
        spills over the window tram
      accompanied by the murmured ache
      of oncoming rain

Lance Covert
Richland, Washington

Jonah Revisited

Jonah
Jonah
Why do you run?
Your God got too much mercy?
My God's an angry one
Like a reverse Jonah
I, too, run
Down into the depths
Of my own waywardness
I sink
In inexorable mercy
God sends a fish
Three days I wait in this smelly grave
Like Jonah
I find a hardness in God's mercy
And a mercy in His hardness
When I start to sing
The One I fled finds me
And the tomb becomes a womb

Teresa Burleson
Fort Worth, Texas

Despair

The shadows are deep in this valley tonight,
it's shrouded with mist and with fog.
I quake as I walk on this narrowing path
that borders a deep murky bog.

I smell the decaying old logs on the edge
all covered with mosses and fern.
I cling to the dripping wet sides of the cliff
with terror and anguish I yearn for the
sunshine and laughter I knew on the hill
where grasses and bright flowers grew.
I long for the days when we sat in the sun
when our life and our love was new.

Remember the nights on the top of the hill
when our friends were young with us too,
and we danced in the light of a full bright moon
that made diamonds and pearls of the dew?

Now the fiddler's music is no longer heard,
and the dancers have all gone away.
The years have passed and I've wandered down
   here
where it's cold at the noon of the day.

There's no one to answer me when I call
I walk in this valley alone.
The only sound that my heart can hear
is the drip of the fog on the stone.

Mary Rauch
Morehouse, Missouri

Loneliness

On an early morning darkened street,
   An aging prostitute lags along.
Cigarette dangling from crimson lips,
   In her brain, an opiated song.
The unrhythmic click of stilted heels,
   Trudging the rain-soaked walk.
There are few tricks this late in life,
   No one with whom to talk.

The wino leans his port-fogged head
   Against the cold hard brick.
A light gray haze now dulls his brain,
   But soon will make him sick.

An old man rattles a trash can lid,
   In search of alley treasures.
The wealth of corrugated tins,
   Supplying his only pleasures.

A policeman in an all-night diner,
   Sitting languidly on tattered seat,
Bemoaning the solitary boredom
   Of his lonely, pre-dawn beat.

The city, the cold hard city,
   With a thousand lost tomorrows.
Every alley, every street,
   An avenue of sorrows.
The pulse beat of a million souls,
   Oblivious to each other's pain.
Washed down the glittering gutters
   By the all-dissolving rain.
Dying, living, being born,
   Each man in his own cocoon.
Passing down the lonely street,
   And gone, but all too soon.

James Frazer
Flandreau, South Dakota

Loneliness Within

The old lady —
   She flickers her eyelids so!
Like the flapping wings of a dying fly,
Like a trembling heart that near death does lie,
The old lady —
   She flickers her eyelids so.

Too much sorrow has she seen.
Too much loneliness, cut off from her kin.

Blot out the image of a cold world of selfish beings;
A flicker that shuts the dreary soul within.
The old lady —
   She flickers her eyelids so!

Tapendu K. Basu
Bourbonnais, Illinois

The Shadow

I saw a shadow on the wall,
A branching, twisting image.
It seemed to grow before my eyes,
A leaping, growing visage.

A ghostly, living shadow
reaching up to breathe.
Growing in the darkness
on the stony wall conceived.

It was a dying shadow
on the stony garden wall.
A graven, twisted image,
soon gone beyond recall.

Vernelia Jobe
Endeavor, Wisconsin

The Worst

The worst is not feeling anything about it,
struggling to get in touch with something;
that seem just out of reach.
Strangely it's better to feel the sorrow,
than to put on a smile and wait for tomorrow;
to feel the pain like an overdose,
overwhelming, near comotose;
with the burden of unsaid thoughts.

Jon Bush
Cambridge, Massachusetts

Disappointments

Is this what the passing of time has done
    after thrusting the knife so often
the blade has become a bit dull
    — one hardly winces at its coming
still, silently praying it will never hurt
    more than the last time
there is some security in the familiar.

Sally Hull Wiebe
Derby Kansas

Oft' Times

Sometimes sitting and thinking
affects the mind much like drinking —
The mind gives way to the inebriate heart
and the ways of the mind and body quickly apart.

The soul begins to cry;
      the body feels it is to die . . .
The mind begins to doubt;
      what the tears are all about . . .

Paul Lee Thomas, II
Woodruff, South Carolina

Hopelessness

At the end of the line is a corner
In the middle of a triangle is a square
By the rectangle lies a circle
Will you find them? Do you care?

At the end of the road there's a wall
From the darkness comes no light
By the river stand no trees
No one puts up a fight.

At the end of life there's no hope
In the middle of death you die
No one is willing to help you
They all just pass you by.

Tammy Lyman
Bolivar, Missouri

The Book is Ours

The book is ours to hold, peruse
    At will, leaf through its golden pages
Tenderly. How shall we choose
    To master it? In easy stages,
Seeking word by word the scheme
    Its author once was dreaming of?
Or hungrily devour the theme
    In one bright evening of love?

The book is ours; there is no need
    For haste to study its designs —
This hour we are content to read
    Between * * * * * the lines.

Pauline Grey
Dodge City, Kansas

Knowledge

The match touches the wick,
a flame springs to life, quavering
slightly, but growing steady as
it becomes a shape unto itself.
It can bend or be shaped,
transformed without putting it
out. From one candle to another
the flames continues on eternally,
lighting some corner of darkness.

Deborah J. Clark
Ingalls, Kansas

Inspiration

In the bathroom, in the car,
doesn't matter where you are,
even in your bed at night;
inspiration comes like second sight.
But try to write some special time,
whether it be prose or rhyme;
do you ever bite the lead?
Wish you'd had a nap instead?
In the night or in the morning,
inspiration gives no warning.
Easy Come. Easy go.
Do you ever find it so?

Esther Edleman
Lost Nation, Iowa

This Poet's Prayer

No amount of thought
Put into this poem
Is going to help,
For once again
As I get the urge to write,
(Oh, how I wish I were a poet),
I discover
I'm no Robert Frost, nor
Another Shakespeare, nor
Wordsworth,
Oh, Lord, either teach me to write
Or break the point on my pencil
So I will no longer
Insult the paper on which I write.

Karen E. Thomas
Aberdeen, Maryland

For Emily Dickinson
(who did not "cross her father's ground")

One aspect of the arts had paused
until a gentle scribe
looked from New England's ledge
to see the soul endure above the toys.
>   Her skills were first to measure
>   emotion's width and depth
>   by fireside light.

For tension, wit, "the velvet heads of birds"
small stanzas wrote themselves
to fill the hand-sewn pages.
Her fragile lines clipped down to classic clause
to gain from hymnal cadence.
She was so much at home
a quiet Monday morning brought a train
roaring into rhyme.
Her choice of cloister sent
transcendent gifts from Amherst.

Darrell H. Bartee
Wichita, Kansas

Writing

The day-dream continues
as the author downs his brandy
in a room
he has survived in
four days.
No one can acknowledge
his working
no one would understand
his simple needs —
to stand in the aisle
of a store,
sit thru a church service,
buy a quarter's worth of candy
and feel the pressure
of the clerk's hand
placing the change
in his hand.

David Ross
Dubuque, Iowa

Pinesol

AM
FM
UHF
VHF
CB
Short wave
Long wave
medium wave
aerosols and smog
and microwave
I open the cabin window
and breathe a lung full
of my friend's clean free
mountain air
pine perfumed sweet scented
Why are they all dying?

Chema Ude
Riverside, California

Supermarketing in the '80s . . .
What's Up, Doc?

Cigarettes don't stand alone as a line to overlook.
The slaps against a lot of things would fill a good-sized book:
Bacon has its nitrites. There's cholesterol in meats,
Chemicals in produce and tooth decay in sweets.
Saccharin is hazardous, so are all food dyes of red.
Dangers lurk in all our foods, including eggs and bread.
The salt in soups and canned goods is a real bad thing to eat.
You can't trust any cereals — not oats, nor corn nor wheat.
In soft goods there are perils, too, like tris in kiddies' clothes,
And tampons are a villain, just as every woman knows.
Health and beauty aids they say can wreck your health and beauty,
So reading every label is a time-consuming duty.
Most deli foods are fatty, and all fast foods are the pits
The supermarket, it would seem, is like a wartime blitz.

If all scare stories are the truth, and charges aren't just cynical,
The supers surely ought to add new sections that are clinical.
The staff expansions, natur'ly, will put a squeeze on purses
As stores find out they have to add nutritionists and nurses.

Cholm G. Houghton
Glen Ellyn, Illinois

Contemplation

The season is upon us
Mother, Father, brethren, friends.
When we seriously consider
By what means we reap our ends.
This vast, glorious, all giving
land we claim
lies so very unsuspecting
as the demons take their aim;
Power, greed, pomposity —
waste without a care
Ah, but yes there is —
there is a rumbling there
nestled in the abdomen
of hunger and despair.
The populace is stirring,
searching silent everywhere
for one solitary answer
but one answer all must share.
We look to our electorates
as they stand to take the floor —
speak for hours lightly skirting
what our souls seek — implore.
Yet we blindly follow
up another dead end street,
chide ourselves for fools we are
and hastily retreat.

What we fail to comprehend;
It's His will thru us be done
and sitting on our laurels
Nary a battle has been won.
We laud and praise our forefathers
for what they fought about
while the very flame for which they shone
is quickly dying out.
Freedom! we say. Independence! we shout
What a curious phenomenon — for now

we have a need, we ask the government.

We dump our waste in our great waters
then regret when we can't fish,
rape our land of all its brush
and mutilate our trees —
use tons of chemicals our
fat, soft palms to grease.
We burn staggering amount of
gas and oil to keep us off our feet
and wonder why we're tired and flabby
waistlines less than neat.

Insects — spray them
Feel discomfort — take a pill
and so bogged down with busies
fail to notice how our Springs
have grown so still —
bereft of bird and beast once so
abundant everywhere.

We're nervous and distrustful
of everyone about
and struggle with our problems
searching ever for an out.

Our lives are overflowing
with disposables and trash.
The very air we breathe
full of chemicals, and ash.

The undeniable truths
are obvious to all;
Will we gather up our strength
seek the answers, act or fall!

J. Kay Lowe
Spirit Lake, Iowa

Budget Cuts

It will be there in the morning when you waken
listening for an explanation of your trembling
   shoulders
and the tears on your cheek.
It will be there with each mention of
next fiscal year and Individual Retirement
   Accounts
and unused sick leave.
It will be there when you look at the clock
and remember the daily routines are almost over.
It will be there each time you make a mistake
to remind you that you were inessential.
It will be there in the eyes of you friends and
   enemies,
the unmentioned subject behind each
   conversation,
the unasked questions about how you are taking it.
It will be there in the way you stiffen your chin and
   raise
your shoulders, hoping pride will compensate for
   being cut.
How many millions have played that game since
   the days
of the monarchs without a throne and the bankrupt
   aristocracy?
How could they worry about where the next dollar
   was
coming from with their soul in danger?
If you are fortunate enough, or unfortunate enough
to see the client's need for you is in their eyes,
   and to be
haunted by the specters of a thousand clients who
   have trusted you,
then you will be wise to call on what is left of your
   strength
and integrity, and answer each phone call with the
   same
freshness and vitality you had on the first day of
   work.

Linda Black Curtis
Urbandale, Iowa

Portraits

ROY BARLAG, 66, is a retired Lutheran pastor and professor. He enjoys gardening, fast walking, and composing light verse. He is a native Hoosier, but most of his adult life has been spent in Texas, Oklahoma and Kansas....**NONI BOOKBINDER BELL,** 23, is a mother of a 4-year old daughter. "I've been writing since I was able to hold a pen. I work part time as a bookkeeper, which is the opposite of being a poet. I've had many poems published, a few paid for. I live on a small farm. I'm presently working on a novel.". ..**KATHLEEN ELA** is a farm wife living in southeast Wisconsin who has always enjoyed writing, although raising 5 children and helping with an apple orchard business have not left her much time. . . . **MARTHA K. GRAHAM** has the distinction of being published in all five CSS Publications poetry anthologies. . . .**ELAINE D. HARDT** is a third grade teacher and the author of *Spare Minute Sparklers, Four Minute Fun for Parent & Child, I. Q. Exercises* (co-author), and *Stories from Beyond the Double Rainbow.* On the board of directors of Arizona Authors Association, she's is demand as a speaker on written and verbal communication. . . . **ANN A. JOHNSON** is a Spanish and English teacher, artist and craftsperson. "I love to travel, and write. I also like the outdoors It is often easier for me to write my feelings than to say them." . . . **ROBERT A. JULIUS,** 47, is a free-lance writer and photographer who has worked as a news reporter and public relations man. He started writing poetry five years ago while studying with Elaine Schweizer; he hopes to publish a book of his poems and photographs someday. **JUDY KEYSER** was born and raised in Illinois but has lived in Iowa for 4 years. She attended Drake University where she took classes in creative writing & poetry. She has been writing poetry for 10 years, and this is her second publication. An interest in nutrition has led to employment at a health food store. . . .**JOHN LEWIS LOZES,** 31, is a poet, playwright and dramatic actor currently working on art forms which fuse communications, dramatic art and music. Jogging, tennis and camping are his hobbies. . . .**MARSHA A. MITCHELL,** 33, mother of 3, is a legal secretary for a utilities company in Centerville. Besides writing poetry, she enjoys writing stories and hopes to begin work on a book soon. **CARMIE PEINTNER** is a farm wife and proud grandmother of 5. "My former husband, my own gambler, was the inspiration for my poem." . . . **HELEN E. RILLING** is a grandmother who enjoys flowers, sewing and reading. She writes both prose and poetry, and believes that putting the right words together is the ultimate joy. . . . **BOB SUMMERS** is a music teacher and composer who is now thoroughly enjoying having his first lyric, without music, published.

Portrait

From a distance
your decided limp comes toward me,
bearing your thick-shouldered body
as if it were too heavy a burden.

Closer,
the unevenness disfiguring your forehead
relaxes into a smile of recognition.

How your body ill-favors you!

You told me one, candidly,
how you have always despised your body,
how you wish you could climb out of it
and leave it empty somewhere.

You have thought of it,
but that would be death,
and you love life.
You smiled when you said
that half a century should have been long enough
to accustom oneself to living
in almost any kind
of shell.

Your blue, incredibly long-lashed eyes
look at me out of your vast intelligence.

Your eyes.
They are the only visible clue
to the deep-flowing ocean of beauty within you,
where irresistible surges of talk
dredge up all manner of beautiful things
that you leave lying about
for people to find
and take up
and hold
and carry away.

Others, as I do,
examine them at leisure,
turning them over and over with delight,
these exotic, luminous, perfectly-shaped treasures
from your beautiful and perfect depths.

Martha K. Graham
Macomb, Illinois

The Rapist

The whisper of jean-clad legs awoke me
To the early morning's misty coldness.
A knee pressed hard against my supple thigh.
He knelt on the bed and laid a bare arm
Across my throat. I gasped for breath to ease
The pain of airless lungs and feigned sound sleep.
Terror gripped my body. He tore away
My silken gown and gently smoothed my skin.
I smelled tobacco and sensed his maleness.
Frantic movements signaled to my numbed mind
His disrobing. I tensed every muscle
For the coming torture. I was helpless
To halt the debauchery of my body.

He sobbed aloud. Released his gripping hold
Dived through the open window and made off.
I struggled up and fought back the blackness
As long waves of nausea washed over me.
My hand touched something lying on the bed.
I opened an embossed leather wallet.
In the dim light of the street lamp I looked
With horror into a familiar face.

Why? Oh my, God! Why?

Helen E. Rilling
Auburn, Illinois

A Couple of Swingers

The porch swing moved lazily,
back and forth,
pushed gently by the wrinkled,
cracked toe of his old black slipper.
My feet, however, dangled,
never coming close to the ground.

He was quite old, tall, wizened,
sporting a snow white mustache.
His movements were slow, deliberate,
always aided by a homemade cane
which hung over the arm of the swing.
The look in his eye was nostalgic, yellowed,
like scotch tape in a scrapbook.

I was very young, small, dark haired,
innocent, so naive and trusting,
especially of him and his boundless knowledge.
We glided silently, he and I,
my tiny hand safely enclosed
in his clawlike, shaky old hand.

Together we watched the butterflies
of summer flit effortlessly
around grandma's front porch geraniums.
As they departed, his feeble grasp tightened.
His rheumy old eyes searched,
looked deeply into my young and eager face.

Then, and again together, we giggled,
my old Uncle Charlie and I.

Marsha A. Mitchell
Centerville, Iowa

New Pupil

Muffled little body
blown in stiffly captive
on a November gust
a tightly wrapped secret
in thin brown jacket
silent stare frosting the room
When our friendship warms you
and the layers are peeled
what will we find?

Elaine D. Hardt
Phoenix, Arizona

The Clown Crier

The Clown Crier walks the streets
And calls the hour.
With each joke he tells,
All's well, all well . . . .

People secure in their houses
Stay behind their lighted windows
Knowing the Clown Crier
Will alert them to laughter.

Clown, hiding in his role,
Stays behind his grease paint
Knowing the crooked smile
Will hide the screaming pain.

What's the hour, Clown Crier?
What's the joke, Clown Crier?
Are we safe, Clown Crier?
Make us laugh, Clown Crier.

Ann Johnson
Litchfield, Minnesota

Memory

I am a dried husk
eaten by fire ants —
tossed by winds of despair.
A young girl saunters by,
green with youth and hope.
I watch her from skeletal sockets.

Kathleen Ela
Rochester, Wisconsin

The Way Bill Is

riding down the road
seashore traffic racing, like agitated hearts
look there — old man bent, a willow
hovered over his flattened tire
deflated hopes
cars blurred in the hot salty sun
Bill sees the gaggle of ancient ladies in the car
sighing, he made the U turn
where the graveyard-white slab median broke
i cursed softly
thinking of sand and hot dogs
but i watched in awe as he pats the old man's
 shoulder
with swift pumps of his strong arms
jacks up the frazzled Ford
gray ladies gaping at his tattoos
he slings the tire into place and it's flat
stifles a groan when the tire iron went through his
 shoe
we drove to the gas station
where he inflated the worn monument to a million
 miles
while a beagle sniffed his shoe . . .

as he turned the last lug
the old man tried to press crumpled bill to his
 hand
eyes shining grateful tears
no thank you sir, i didn't mind
a fine young man, i wish you were a grandson of
 mine
we left throwing dust, smiling and sweating
i waved at the man
my hands swooped like suntanned seagulls
i looked sideways at him, secretly
from behind my dark shades
thinking — how can you be so good, when things,
 for you,

have been so bad
he could have been my grandfather, Bill says
reading my thoughts
as if they were balloons hanging in the humid air...

Noni Bookbinder Bell
Vincentown, New Jersey

Jeanne

Eagerly I walk the same long city block
In anticipation of seeing once again
The portrait of my favorite little girl
In the front window of a picture studio.
With merry blue eyes twinkling, she sits
Beneath a lacy white chapeau.
I'm hypnotized. Her sweet beauty prints itself
Upon my mind. It must last until next year.
Farther back along one wall I glimpse
Another of her portraits as a flower girl.
A blue veil tilts over one mischievous eye
As she leans — so weary with grown-up affairs —
On the fingertips of one tiny white-gloved hand.
I realize she must be all of twenty now.
But I remember her best in her lacy hat
Of white and the filmy circlet of blue.
Again this year memories tug at my heart
For one more reunion. I stop before the windows.
They're empty. The blank glass mirrors my
Sorrowful and aging face. I press close.
Old cartons and loose debris clutter the floor.
I search the windows again and again
For the little girl in the pretty hat,
Jeanne.

Helen E. Rilling
Auburn, Illinois

Bird Lady

She sings, her softened feathers
    folded neatly across her
    rounded breast of heather.
She coos and plucks unruly items
    from her life and watches as they
    float silently to rest at her feet.
She bobs, in an attempt to escape
    from the confining cage
    she so freely entered.
She speaks, twittering constantly
    about nothing, even though
    there is no one to listen.
She flies, around in circles,
    gaining height, then suddenly
    plummets to where she began.
She shakes her head, clears her mind,
    then starts all over again.

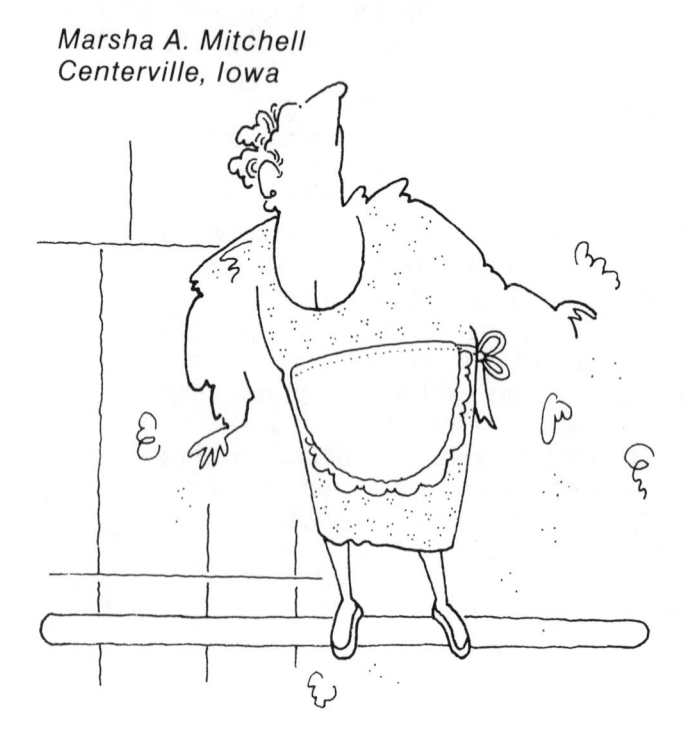

Marsha A. Mitchell
Centerville, Iowa

Jessie

The woman
down the street
keeps cats.
The grey one
with the green eyes
is in the window
always,
like Portland fog
looking out
and dissolving
into mist.
She walks at noon,
everyday
down the cracked sidewalk
slowly, with a cane.
She wears the same
black overcoat
even in summer.
She stops and tells
stories about the old country,
Scotland
in her broken English
you can imagine her
there in Edinburgh
young with a quick voice.
In back, by her garden
she bends to pick a marigold
while the cats hide
behind the ivy.

Judy Keyser
Des Moines, Iowa

My Sombero
(The Image Maker)

I bought me a hat; a Western hat.
Who could find anything wrong with that?
There's no reason to object
But it's changed the image I project.

My friends no longer call me Roy;
They treat me like a "good ol' boy."
Even when they use my name
It simply doesn't sound the same.

And it's strange as it can be,
The effect this hat has had on me.
When I put on my new sombrero
I start to act like an old ranchero.

I've put aside my walking-cane;
Now I swagger like Big John Wayne.
I ought to return it to the store
'Cause I hardly feel like me no more.

But I'm afraid it's now too late.
"Why?" you ask. Let me elucidate:
I already feel ten feet tall
And have acquired a Western drawl.

My taste in music has begun to change;
I now enjoy "Home on the Range."
Don't wanna hear no rock-n-roll band;
I'd rather sing "I'm an Old Cowhand."

As for food, I'd rather by far
Have a thick steak than caviar.
Dress to dine out? I prefer plain jeans.
Gimme Bar-B-Q and a plate of beans.

You'll see me no more in fancy suits;
I'll wear plaid shirts and cowboy boots.
My sombrero has put me under a hex.
From now on you can call me "Tex!"

Roy Barlag
Blue Springs, Missouri

Stephane's Song

Your song was alive with perpetual youth
when it came to me out of speeding darkness
and I was reminded of the cuts done with Django
in Paris before the war.

Lines that bubbled and rolled and soared
elbowed their way happily, even crazily,
through my side.
And a million sparks splashed about,
crashing into my soul, causing me to shiver,
to smile.

Then there was smoke as your bow put fire
to "April" and a mind's-eye picture
of Pass and Orsted Pederson busting their strings
just trying to keep up,
not knowing as I do
that no one's going to catch you.

Robert A. Julius
Centerville, Iowa

The Safecracker's Dream

In a rooming house in downtown Chicago
Henry Logan sits dripping sweat on the dirty floor
His life's dream was shattered by a beautiful
    woman named Cookie
He is now a loner

His flat contains a small cot and a broken chair
    which have crept into his mind

He cannot get the sleep he needs while the
     thought of seeing anyone frightens him
Henry gropes for a single idea
Diamonds, furs and money to waste can tantalize
     Cookie he cannot stop thinking and suddenly
     he's planning a heist working it over and over
     when an uncontrollable action dangles Henry
     from the side of a skyscraper forty-six stories
     up exhausted from climbing

At last to the roof top of the Hotel Rix he dashes to
     an air duct and squeezes down its shaft to the
     vault on floor six
Wildly he kicks a screen-covered vent then falls
     hard to the floor

Convinced that he's dead he sorely rolls over and
     sees the hotel cache across the room
He spins the dials quickly "click" the safe
     springs open for a moment he sees his only
     chance to regain his cherished prize when a
     bell rings out striking his ears instantly his
     emotions pop and vanish

With nothing worth seeing, tasting, hearing,
     smelling or touching
Henry sits alone day after day, year after year
     quietly babbling into one corner of a small
     square room
I've lost you forever my dearest love

John Lewis Lozes
Iowa City, Iowa

Marianne

A soul that claimed no other world
    but this her own
    of friends and talk and fun
    that came without thought;

A love of beauty
    that came without design
    but just to know that it was there;

Simplicity that held all
    that's great of large and small;

A lovely lady yet to bloom,
    but gone . . .

Bob Summers
Iola, Kansas

The Gambler

Who ever risks more,
    trusts more,
        hopes more,
  than the farmer?
He bets all he earns,
    all he can borrow,
        on tomorrow.
The odds are against him,
    so is the weather,
        and the bugs.
He is up early,
  works late,
    rotates crops,
        and tempts fate.
And feeds a hungry world.

Carmie Peintner
Spearville, Kansas

From the Corner...

LAURRE BREMAN, a graduate in human behavior from Grand View College, tries to incorporate into her writing some insights gleaned from her college experience. "When I write, I endeavor to directly touch the reader's feelings." Seeking publication for her first novel, she spends her spare hours working on another. "I love to create." . . . **DORIS T. BROKAW** tangles with weeds and the elements during the spring, summer and fall . . . but reserves the winter months for study and poetry writing. . . . **LINDA BLACK CURTIS** is a political volunteer, a social worker and a union member. Poetry helps put it all together. . . . **MARTHA K. GRAHAM's** biographical sketch appears in Chapter 1. . . . **TRACY GRANDY,** 17, is a high school senior in Cedar Falls, Iowa. She enjoys writing, ballet and tennis. She has had one previously published poem. . . . **JEAN KENNEDY,** who writes fiction and nonfiction as well as poetry, teaches writing courses at the University of Northern Iowa. She has worked for newspapers, professional journals, and is the mother of 3. . . . **MAX D. MAXON,** a University of Iowa graduate, is the father of 4 and has 4 grandchildren. A lifelong Webster City resident, he is a 41-year employee of *Daily Freeman-Journal,* serving as editor and columnist. He writes poetry on occasion for his daily column, "Amblin' with Maxi." . . . . **DIANNA TORSON RANDALL** enjoys horses and horseback riding. She is a black belt in Japanese Shotokan Karate and runs a commercial beekeeping operation in Iowa and South Dakota with her husband and son. . . . **HELEN E. RILLING's** bio appears in Chapter 2. . . . **LYNNE PROCTOR SANCKEN,** 32, although born and raised in Pennsylvania, feels more at home here in the Midwest. She has been writing poetry since she was 9 and tries to be ever mindful of God as its source. Lynn and her husband have 2 young children. . . . **JANET SMITH,** 32, is a back-to-earther who lives in an old country house. A painter, she has shown her work in Oklahoma and Canada. . . . **JOHN SHARSMITH** enjoys hiking and cross-country skiing in the Wyoming backcountry. Inspiration for his poetry comes from personal experiences, nature and dreams. He has been writing poetry about four years. . . .

Spectrum
Continued from page 2 . . .

been writing poetry since age 7. She is an active member of several writing & poetry organizations and entertains thoughts of putting together a volume of her poems. She loves anything to do with nature and has a special fondness for the sea. . . . **PAUL LEE THOMAS, II,** 21, is an English educational major at the University of South Carolina at Spartanburg. He is a struggling young writer of both poetry & prose and a believer that all men/women are poets. He is also forever indebted to e.e. cummings. . . . **CHEMA UDE,** 34, is an urban planner from Eastern Nigeria currently living in Riverside, California. He is a free-lance photojournalist with several published poems and short stories and awards in photography. He enjoys tennis & auto racing, and is currently working on his first novel and book of poems. . . . **SALLY HULL WIEBE,** mother of 4 children, has a variety of interests, although her interest in poetry has been avid since her high school days. She often begins writing at 2 a.m. and would like to become somewhat more disciplined. . . . **THE "BANQUET POEM"** resulted from a late-night group effort by guests who attended the second annual CSS Publications Poetry Day & Awards Banquet on December 10, 1981, in Ames, Iowa. Contributors to the poem included Rebecca Bell, Doris & Emerson Brokaw, Myrna Fridley, Amy Nyman, Carol S. & Robert M. Owen, Kathleen Peirce, Rusti & William P. Riddle, David Ross, C. Sherman Severin, Sarah P. Simmons, Nancy Smith and Curt L. Sytsma.

From the corner

I see the moon, full and still
on this winter afternoon,
a snowball tossed aloft
and caught there
like a ghost shadow in a photograph.
Startled, I pause with my car
longer that the stop sign warrants,
and my suprise rises,
an unexpected hope,
which waxes, wanes,
and then comes back, rising like
this impact-battered moon.
The windshield is in between,
but I do see it there.

The knowing turns with me,
an afterimage on my retina.
So I carry the fullness home
as I might a fragrant melon
found in January.

Jean Kennedy
Waterloo, Iowa

Honorable Mention

The Midwest (in Five Parts)

I. Illinois

The earth is skinned
each spring
spreading its arms black
as far back
as they can go.

II. Summerpoem for Greg

Summer comes.
Your skin holds the sun
like ripe wheat.

III. Mississippi

The river in Iowa
is the color of rusty blood
pumped from the heart-
land. On the dock,
my feet in the water,
I could take root here.

IV. Goodland, Indiana

The women nest on porches.
Their hands grow gentle
peeling peaches
into wide laps.

V. Route 40/ Fall Crops/ Inheritance

Blond as my son,
the corn has gone
to seed (gone).

The beans have been taken,
already dried to the same shade
as old blood.

There,
and there,
the big earth-muscles

lie bare again,
open to wind and fire.
My husband's hands open.

They still carry
the flesh of the land
that keeps them fallow.

Lynn Proctor Sancken
Sidney, Illinois

Second Place Poem

This Quiet Lane

In the crispy dew of early morn
as drowsy nature woke to reign
the dawn of day was yet unborn
as I strolled down this quiet lane

The hazy fog near kissed the earth
anticipating sunrays claim
to vanquish, waken and give birth
as I strolled down this quiet lane

A bronze-like sky peeked through at me
to shame the fog with sun's disdain
to purge, erase, break sun-rays free
as I strolled down this quiet lane.

The brilliance of this infant day
a newborn babe her life to feign
could I, excitement hold at bay?
as I strolled down this quiet lane

Mine eyes devoured, feasted, drank
on miracles of wind-blown grain
like ocean waves that rose and sank
as I strolled down this quiet lane

Off to my right on pine stump fence
entwined sky climbing, light to gain,
green grapevines with their leaves so dense
as I strolled down this quiet lane

The songbirds joined from every tree
to harmonize in sweet refrain
my soul cried out so merrily
as I strolled down this quiet lane

A vibrant sound quite startled me
till into view an eerie crane,
to vanish just as speedily,
as I strolled down this quiet lane

The fragrance of the wild bloom
enhanced from nectar of the rain
admonished I should not leave soon
as I strolled down this quiet lane

The grandeur of all nature's things
abound within and shall remain
I said "farewell", till my life brings
me down this quiet lane again

Joseph Avery Sweet
Traverse City, Michigan

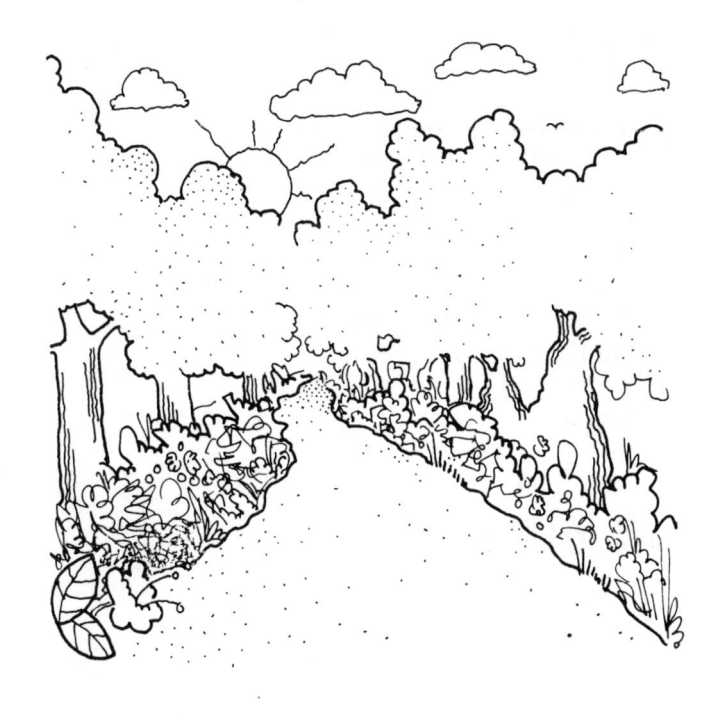

Skipping Stones

When I was a boy I liked skipping stones,
Selecting just the right one, round and flat,
   from a seemingly endless supply,
Then bending low, sending it sailing
   with a side-sweep of the arm,
Watching it skip and bounce, and counting
   the times.
We had contests, my friend and I, for skips,
   or distance or size or aim.
Ever try to skip a six-pounder?
The trick was to keep them from curving
   at the end,
The stone just sliding along the surface,
   so it didn't bounce at all,
Then it sank, and we could see it wink
   in the clear green water.
Ripples would spread, of a calm morning,
   til they'd join, like beads in a necklace.
It was a celebration of life: of sun,
   cicadas and summer.
But was I there to skip stones, or to listen to the
   silence,
Smell the damp logs, sun-dried algae,
Walk on warm sand, and feel the wind tousle my
   hair?
I still like to skip stones, though I think we threw
   all the good ones away.

John Sharsmith
Jackson, Wyoming

Honorable Mention

Cleaning Fish

A shimmer of scales moves iridescently
in porch light, flying over nicked knuckles,
falling to grass milky white.

Detached, a rod jerked to deep water,
we follow the blade blooming belly to vent—
fingers pluck viscera like harp strings, cut
deeply into spine, searching for blood pockets.

I, father's sissy, prepare pliers for a peeling of skin.
You laugh at the pale bladders of my eyes,
watch the hesitant scooping of entrails into
    newspaper,
the scurry between bushes to bury my dead.

A white enamel basin is pink with our washing.
Outside the window, a blue-veined moon
is caught in a criss-cross of nesting trees.
Dreams float like corks, fish frenzied in gunny
    sacks.

Your eyes are glossy as shells and empty, blindly
sensing that resonance of the sea, that catch:
the nearness of the day when a furling of scales
will come, and these hands will hold living things
turned ruby in porch light, taking blood as their
    own.

Glen Enloe
Independence, Missouri

First Place Poem

Cathedral Chimes

Cathedral chimes,
And words that rhyme,
And leaves that whisper in the wind.

Quiet talks,
And silent walks,
And weeping willows that bend.

Autumn sun,
And waters that run,
And pastel colors that blend.

Swallows that fly,
And mother's pie,
And a basket of clothes to mend.

Poplar trees,
And shelling peas,
And old letters from a friend.

Tomatoes warm from the vine,
The smell of pine,
May these things never end.

Janet Smith
Tahlequah, Oklahoma

Help

Indians! Where are you going.
Coyote, Wolf, Fox! Where are you now.
You brothers—
Chased, maimed, destroyed—
The ones who could have told us how.

Dianna Randall
Brookings, South Dakota

Do You Believe?

I don't believe in ghosts; perhaps I should,
For here in Iowa stand ghosts of wood.
The ghosts I'm speaking of — have no alarm —
Are empty homes that stand on many a farm.

Their glassless eyes stare out as you pass by,
And if the wind is right you hear a cry,
"Where has my family gone? Please send them back!"
(It's just the wind that sounds through chimney crack.)

What has that sagging home seen through the years?
Some happy newlyweds, with hopes and fears,
Achieved a heavenly joy right here on earth,
A joy 'twas added to with children's birth.

Or did depression hit with 10-cent corn,
Burned in the stove each wintry morn?
Did typhoid fever strike from that old well,
And turn that heavenly joy to tragic Hell?

If those old walls could speak, what tales we'd hear
Of family love or strife, of gloom or cheer?
Those former tenants now are scattered far.
I don't believe in ghosts — yet there they are!

Max Maxon
Webster City, Iowa

To An Old House

Built long ago for a bride
brought from the distant safe and settled east
to this wild river,
still you stand as straight
as you first stood in eighteen thirty-four.

Your builder, young and sure of hand and eye,
shaped the stone, square-nailed the rising frame,
whimsically mortared a geode into one wall
and dreamed you white and lovely as a bride.

Abby, only twenty, and Cyrus, older,
the two of them have slept beneath their stones
more than a hundred years, at Riverside,
next Gordons and Cochrans, neighbors, too, in
  life.

But safe within your walls the dream lives on,
moves bride-like through the square, high-
  ceilinged rooms,
walks the wide verandas all around
and wanders the dooryard garden, full of bloom.

Only he who built so lovingly
could ever own you, but we found you here
alone and lonely, by the river road,
and stepped inside, and knew you held a dream.

We dressed you once again in shining white,
and when you stood so tall and beautiful,
we veiled you in white, lacy bridal wreath
and heaped a flower garden in your arms.

Martha K. Graham
Macomb, Illinois

Sun-Warmed Memory

In the middle of a great strawberry patch in the sun,
a small child plucking heart-shaped, seed-covered
   berries,
popping them not into the bowl,
but sampling the succulent, sour-sweet goodness;
Biting one, it squishes, releasing scarlet nectar.
The child returns to the house, strawberry-stained,
   happy,
bowl empty, stomach full.

Tracy Grandy
Cedar Falls, Iowa
Age 17

Gone

This house is fallen from grace with its broken
railing pulling stubbornly from the cement porch
and paint peeled down to the grey shell.
The sink and tub are ready to be retired.
The stove and refrigerator came second hand
from a larger house. They are broken now;
castoffs from another time.
Haul them away, and exorcise with them
the memories of many cousins
performing an appendectomy on my teddy bear.
We are all play acting in our long garments;
pretending that winter will never
pack ice chips around the garbage cans.
My ancient aunt lies tranquil and resigned
in her sterile bed wearing lipstick
while nurses tend her, and a roommate
complains that the laundry shrunk her sweater.
The October wind is cold today
The gas is turned low. I will
wonder at night about the welfare
of the water pipes in the empty cold house.
My aunt speaks only of going home,
where she will never go again.
I believe unequivocally that she loves
that small house; scene of her loneliness
and pain. The house did not love her back.
It was spiteful instead. The roaches
and mice made derelict companions.
The grass grew too fast.
The water bills and power bills exceeded
her bank balance. The food spoiled
in her broken refrigerator.
The roof leaked. Had there not been so
much pain, she would be in her house yet;
free to live without interference.
She waited patiently while
the diseased tissue was cut away.

Ah, house. A political brochure
hangs on your knob today.
Offers to meet your needs with legislation
are too late for this house.
It is time to relocate,
and be taken care of forever.

Linda Black Curtis
Urbandale, Iowa

Foreclosure Sale

In a small country town a few miles to the west
His cardboard suitcase tied with twine and filled
   with clothes
Sits in a back bedroom at Rose's Boardinghouse,
With family pictures and a few mementos.

Once echoing over the broken pasture land
The auctioneer's chant, "going, going, gone," so loud
Is stilled and no one sees the lonely figure clad
In faded denims weave his way among the crowd.

A summer drought, poor prices, and rent much too high.
Foreclosure signs on shed for everyone to see.
"He's broke," they said to each other. "Sad. A good man."
He heard. His old cap's visor bent into a vee.
He was glad Nella was gone. She'd likely be sad.
The children lived in town and seldom returned at all.

Friends and neighbors talked and bid against each other
For his horses, the spade, the pictures off the wall.
Later he walked one last time over the meadow.
His dog curled at his feet as he leaned on a post.

Recalled winter snows that left fields like dominoes,
Summer's ripe wheat, but it was corn shocks he loved most.
The empty house was dark as he looked back toward
The barn and sheds. No milch cow waited at the gate.

"Git up, Shep. Come, Boy. It's time we headed on home.
Nella's cooking supper and we oughtn't be late."

Helen E. Rilling
Auburn, Illinois

Requiem for a General Store

The store is old, and empty now.
Its walls, splintered and cracked, fade
   crookedly into gray obscurity
Against the brown tangle of weeds which
   march in slow triumph
To seek final possession among the clapboards.

A shutter hangs askew, flapping aimlessly
   with the nuances of time;
Hollow darkness peers blankly from
   the broken windows, and the door,
Whose hinges are rust-frozen in weary welcome.

Small rustles and squeaks disturb the silence:
   the snakes and mice,
The new proprietors, eager about their
   business,
Condemning the store more surely than
   the rain-washed notice
Tacked so indifferently to its frame.

Yet, upon its dusty wooden shelves,
   stocked now with mouse-droppings
   and small scuttling things,
The tangy aroma of far-travelled spices
   lays poignant and sharp.
Ancient echoes of laughter and gossip
   waft upon the breeze that whispers in,
And the shadowy sounds of footsteps,
   summer-bare,
Slap wetly on the floorboards,
   a grimy fist trickling sticky sweets.

In the corner, unconcerned with
   here and now,
A spider quietly spins her web,
   building it with the foundation
Of yesterdays gone by.

Laurre Breman
Des Moines, Iowa

Reverie & Wails

Bernard Warehouse
borders the College Street sidewalk.
Years ago errand feet
traveled this familiar street
where the smell of Burley tobacco
prickled the nose.
    Inside the sagging structure
    diagonal streams of sunlight appear
    frozen along the unmarked dusty floor.
    Echoes of auctioneer staccato drones
        mingle
    with vibrations of handcarts — rumbling
    between rows of stacked baskets.
This spring day
I'm standing on the rusting scales,
rocking back and forth, reviving
hardy folks wearing last year
and the year before clothes —
bartering their season's toil
for small reward:
slapping thighs and swapping tales
of still longer times remembered.
    In the summertime busy brooms
    convert the smooth floor
    into a makeshift skating rink:
    Our only music
    the cluster sounds
    of children playing.
    Three long wails: The Fire Station
        siren intrudes!
    It's twelve o'clock noon.

Doris T. Brokaw
Canton, Missouri

Introspection

J. KARYL ARNOLD runs a literary and editorial service. A professional poet-writer, she has been a guest speaker at many writers' conferences. She directs two weekly writing workshops from her home, and has been published in a large variety of markets. . . . **NICHOLAS JAMES ATKINSON,** 32, is an officer with a national real estate investment corporation. His wife Joan is a portrait sculptor. His interests are reading, music, dogs and handguns. . . . **PEG BARRY,** mother of 6 and grandmother of 5, says, "I have always known a thirst for beauty: in words, in poetry, in art, in life and in its individual expression, whether it be someone else's or my own." . . . A graduate of the University of Kansas, **MARGARET MATTHEWS BRADLEY** is a member of Kansas Watercolor Society, Wichita Artists Guild and Kansas Silversmithing and Enamalist Guild. . . . **SUE ANN (LEE) CARDWELL,** 26, has been writing poetry since age 14. She will be attending Ivy Tech School of Technology for computer programming. . . . **R. J. CAYLOR,** 45, has been writing poetry for his own enjoyment since age 10 but only started writing seriously 3 years ago. Until this fall he was unpublished; this is his second published poem. . . . **BILL FORSYTHE** is news director for WEVZ-FM in Fort Wayne, Indiana. He is working on an autiobiography of the unconscious. . . . **LYDIA HARTUNIAN,** 19, is a philosophy-English major at the University of Iowa. Poetry writing is a new expression for her and one she plans to continue throughout her life. . . .

DON HELMSTETTER, 33, is an educator/counselor and a frequent guest speaker for community organizations. He is a consultant to schools and business, giving workshops in the areas of stress, chemical abuse, family & youth concerns. . . . **MICHAEL G. KELLY,** 42, is a communications professional whose interests include film studies, theology and human liberation and development. He is currently an advertising agency creative supervisor, married and the father of 4. . . . **REBECCA DAWN LAKANEN,** 29, is bright-eyed in the presence of poetry. Through sensitive reflection and honesty, she hopes to create something unique that will live after her. . . . **ESTHER MENNEN** is a senior citizen, mother of 3 sons and grandmother of 6, 3 boys and 3 girls. She taught school for 5 years. "Lots of times I compose poetry when I can't sleep at night." . . . **CONSTANCE LEIGH RENTEL,** 32, recently finished her first book of poetry. She has been writing for 5 years but only began sending her work out in January, 1982. Since then, she has had 175 rejections and 48 poems accepted for publication.

JEAN MARIE SCHULTZ is the assistant vice president of a bank near Stillwater and writes poetry for pleasure and perspective. . . . **ANN LYNN SMITH,** 39, is a practicing attorney in Montgomery County, Kansas. She is married, has 5 children and enjoys reading and writing poetry. . . . **BRUCE STANSBERRY,** 38, married, father of 3, is a social work supervisor who enjoys music, sports and friends. He spends much of his spare time composing poetry and songs. This is his first published poem. . . . **GURLEY STARLIN,** 58, lives in a beautiful Christian farming community near Vogel Center, Michigan. She has been writing poetry for many years, and now is able to devote more time to her poetry. She is greatly encouraged by those who enjoy her poetry. . . . **ALICE MACKENZIE SWAIM** is the author of 10 books, numerous brochures and articles, and more than 7,000 published poems; she has received more than 350 national and international awards. A member of many poetry organizations, she has served as contest judge, book reviewer and poetry consultant. . . . **PHYLIS LEE WILLIAMS** has loved and written poetry all of her life. She also enjoys writing both religious and popular songs. Coming from a typically English ethnic background indeed lends to her fervor for writing. "I feel there is a definite need for both a moral as well as a patriotic renaissance due in America." . . . **MILDRED HOPE WOOD** writes her best poetry while traveling with her husband, often writing 50-60 poems and an article or an essay during one trip.

Introspection

I have no place,
unlike
the quiet street at night
that fits so right
its black against
the gleam of grass.

And there is no sense
pretending
that the stars or moon so high
could rock me when I sigh
or understand my dreams.

Like the click in the
close
of a door
somewhere,
sometime
I will find
my place.

Jean Marie Schultz
Stillwater, Minnesota

Reflections of a Wall Flower

Silence . . .
though the room permeates with laughter
and mindless small-talk.
I am alone here;
I prefer it.
The others are not like me,
so I close them out.

Only,
sometimes
I'd like
to try
to join the others.
Do you think
they would close me out
again?

Don Helmstetter
Fairmont, Minnesota

Winter Poem, 1980

Seven years ago last winter,
I willfully shattered the mirror
    of my existence.

Since, I have crawled through the pieces,
trying to create the change I craved.

Ann Lynn Smith
Coffeyville, Kansas

Broken Glass

I've wondered who I am, what I'm like;
Tonight I know. Dim night light
On gray pavement reveals broken glass . . .
Amber-brown, rich-toned, glistening, glimmering,
    gleaming,
Catching the light in a sparkle-dance.
I too am broken glass,
Ground-in, scattered at random,
My lustre lovely, my form fragmented,
Sharp edges scoring the softness of sundown.
Oh, wanderer! Walking at night,
Stopping in the street light glare,
Surveying my shiny specks;
What do you see in your circle of sight?
Am I beautiful, shimmering,
Dotting the darkness in dazzling waste?
Or am I but garbage, man's flung-away refuse
That slaked his thirst once but now I am empty,
    useless . . .
Threatening, treacherous underfoot?
Crunch me or kick me; sweep me into a green
    garbage bag.
Grind me to powder, return me to sand.
Still I will glint and gleam in the light . . .
A tossed-aside vessel in the night . . .
Broken glass.

J. Karyl Arnold
Medina, Ohio

Adrift

It is Evening
Dusk is beginning to fall
Black limbs of elm trees
Trace themselves in lace against the sky.
I wander the streets alone,
Pale lights in windows begin
I glance with unease within
And hurry on.

But why?

No need for haste
No light awaits my coming,
No faint smoke curls from my chimney place.
Am I not walking to delay my homeward way?
Four ugly walls, a bed hard white,
A chair, a table and a light.
My thoughts are mean
My spirit black with rage
At things that be.
And then with fury spent,
I sink with weakness into apathy.
That I should be of those wanderers
No home, no friends, no roots.
I stand bewildered!

Is it that I have lost my place
In this ghastly race?

Margaret Matthews Bradley
Wichita, Kansas

life from the sea

i sit solitary
on a misty shore
rapt in the rhythm
of a pulsating sea
as seagulls soar
and a soft breeze
with salty scent
whispers
of mysteries
from other spheres.
regretting
the trance is spent
by a hermit crab
pirouetting
on this lonely strand
shedding its shell
on the dampened sand
for yet another
hollow
with room to grow.
i rise and follow
for i too must dance
on the sands of time
to perchance
find mine.

peg barry
south braintree, massachusetts

How Many Times

How many times
must I stand on the shore
watching the incoming tide,

Only to find
there is no ship
with my name on its weathered side.

How many times
must I walk the hills
in search of my peace of mind,

Only to find
the treasure I seek
is the treasure I left behind.

How many times
must I wait for the dawn
to bring me the morning light,

Only to find
I have lost my way
in the dark of a moonless night.

How many times
must I fall in love
wearing my heart on my sleeve,

Only to find
I must give of myself
before I can hope to receive.

How many times
must I look for the truth
not knowing where it might be,

Only to find
the beginning of truth
lies in the ending of "Me"

How many times
must I stand all alone
when tyranny spreads o'er the land,

Only to find
that freedom will grow
where strong-minded men take a stand.

How many times
must I act like a man
with a strength I never have known,

Only to find
that acting itself
is the greatest strength I'll ever own.

R. J. Caylor
Jacksonville, Florida

Wide Awake Dreams

Daydreaming in colors of orange
and yellow firelight reflecting
on floor pillows of creme silk
. . . there lies the vision of two
    so close
    they share secrets
    about themselves
    in whispers

Imagining I'm tracing the outline
of his lower lip and knowing again
that incredible awareness of how
    surprisingly smooth
    it feels
    against mine

Remembering that intensity of
feeling when kisses first become
inquiring in their trembling search
    for knowledge
    of one another

Knowing this is but a dream . . .

Wondering why I'm not at least
asleep so that I could
    actively
    participate

Constance Leigh Rentel
Tacoma, Washington

Dreams with a Shadowed Past

*Dreams with a shadowed past,
    Have slowly slipped away.
Visions that will never last,
    Words you never say.

Journeys that will take you far,
    Memories that never end.
Forgotten thoughts upon a star,
    Love that's left with friends.

Lessons that have taught you well,
    Goals you've seldomed reached.
A spirit that inside you dwells,
    All you've been taught, you teach.

Seeing life, through different eyes,
    No judgement has been made.
Finding honesty, without the lies,
    The path for you is laid.

Reaching out for something new,
    You never look behind.
Finding, all along it was you,
    Leaves total peace of mind.

Sue Ann (Lee) Cardwell
Terre Haute, Indiana

Umbrellas

I can remember
when we took our chances,
unbound by convention or rule;
venturing out on a limb in the dark,
indifferent to most ridicule.

We leaped without looking
and wagered our all,
undaunted by unfavorable odds;
free-wheeling shots playing anything goes,
like hobos who dangle from rods.

Sometimes we stumbled
in random directions,
unwary of scheme or design;
like fanciful daredevils trusting to chance
whatever we laid on the line.

We ran from routine
and searched out for adventure
until the years brought a refrain.
And now, we carry umbrellas
in case we get caught in the rain.

Bruce Stansberry
Anderson, Indiana

Windhorse

The child on
the carousel
is me . . .
hair flying free
above a wooden mane.

Nostrils flaired
drawing in
painted wind.

Life is lived
in a circular fashion
astride a circus steed;
taking the same leap
over and over
on a pole fixed to the
canopy of heaven.

Bright pony,
jewelled harness.
Let go the rein.
The ride is
the same.

The child on
the carousel
is mine . . .
eyes fixed
on the future.

The calliope
always draws
an applause
of tears.

Michael G. Kelly
Valley, Minnesota

Honorable Mention

Meditation

The Atlantic soothes
him, wave by wave; a gentle
man, a child of cloud

and sea. Pondering
the timeless lullaby, he
journeys skyward, to

join the slow dance of
ancient stars. There is music
everywhere; light-years

within, and microns
away, it is all the same.
Have you ever trailed

a comet, or felt
one shoot through your hands? Planets
pull, and tides fall . . . Has

heaven always been
so blue? And is this a dream,
or a memory,

Galileo? The
universe glides in, wave by
wave, if you let it.

*Rebecca Lakanen
Negaunee, Michigan*

Emotions in Retrospect

    Emotions are like falling rain,
that nurtures the parched earth.
    They serve our mortal body,
to soothe and cleanse from the moment of birth.

    A drop,
and then a trickle,
    a stream,
and then a flood,
    feelings,
in retrospect,
    free the body,
and purify life's blood.

    For with the hates and passions,
the torments and the fears,
    the sanguine sense of comprehension,
may set free a stream of tears.

    "Oh, eyes of mortal combat,
that betray the weakest urge,
    how can you serve such a fickle master,
and betray the strongest words?"

Phylis Williams
Vinton, Iowa

Unseen Dimensions

All things cannot be measured by the visible
   Love can't
      Intention cannot —
         Nor innocence.

Our eyes cannot perceive
   The secret thoughts
      Untold yearnings —
         Nor smitten conscience.

Neither can we fathom
   Anothers grief
      Heartaches or pain —
         Nor loneliness.

Or can we understand why they are prompted
   To seek a mortal end
      A different path —
         An ease of care.

So can we neither judge
   But our heart only —
      Nor walk the trail they walk
         For each soul has its own journey
            And its own destination.

Gurley Starlin
McBain, Michigan

The Shadow Stone

Sioux legend says a sacred stone
hung from Crazy Horse's neck,

and with this amulet
he passed into the spirit side

at will
and returned at will.

his clothes were pierced by bullets
but the warrior was untouched.

Sioux legend says a sacred stone
hung from Crazy Horse's neck,

but his people are alcoholic phantoms
peddling trinkets and stones.

and if, as legend says,
this world is but a shadow

of the spirit side,
then eternity suffers, too.

Bill Forsythe
Fort Wayne, Indiana

The Face of Truth

I trailed a noble English sheepdog across
A purple-heathered, heathen moor where
One false step away, oblivion
Awaits the unwary traveller, there to join
Immired bones of legionnaires and standard
 bearers
Who centuries before had also lost their way.

Pinnacled in this marshy wilderness of timeless
 memory
A man could lean into the wind,
Hear the battle clash of ancient armies
The magic chant of pagan druid
Gentle tones of curlew call
Lost lamb's plaintiff bleat
The very voice of desolation.

Though King of Beings I knew not the path
So blindly followed I this speechless beast
As it scampered on before. Then low cloud
 enshrouded us.
Damp, inpenetrable, auguring ill what lay ahead.
But still I followed warm and softly padded paws,
Committed to an unerring canine compass.
Twilight fell and as increasing distance stood
 behind
Awesome wonder deeply filled my glowing soul,
Humbled was I by this creature's certain
Knowledge of the Way while Man trudged on
 unknowingly

I stood before a tiny cottage gate, savored for
 a moment
Lovely cherry smoke, Nature's own incense;
And kneeling there upon that sodden heath
I touched the furry face of truth
And understood that simple Faith
Would be the guide along that Narrow Way.

Nicholas Atkinson
St. Charles, Illinois

Hidden Truths

Facades enclose the human race.
Am I to play their game?
Indicted with hypocrisy,
They strive to sing the same.
Yet I, my song so far apart
Can find no piece so grand,
For if I mask the earthly truths
Death beckons in command.
I want the earth, the sun, the sea
Alive in natural air.
Not tainted with the clouds of dark
Whose rain soaks all they wear.
To wipe the script imprinted here
Is task I must not wane,
For if I walk in untrue step
I'll pass my life in vain.
Untimely moments pursue their course
As I in time must march
Along the side of false soldiers
Who stage a patriarch.
Yet, mine like theirs is not so small
Whose grasp they can obtain.
The glories of the wondrous earth
Are none I can contain
Still strive I will 'till endless dawn
Unveil the justice due
And stray away from all that's false
And live in all that's true.

Lydia Hartunian
Cedar Rapids, Iowa

The Light Touch

What matters most
is never to be serious
about important things.
A touch of basil in a casserole—
that can be argued without sense of shame;
the proper vibrancy of color that enhances
a room monotonous with stifling drabness.
There is such range of trivialities
that every mind can ride its hobbyhorse
and stay in place.
But when we bang our heads and daze our eyes
against inevitable urgencies,
reality is far too large for explanation.
We stand like mutes arranged for photographs
as destiny unrolls and time stands still,
and try to comfort with inanities.

Alice Mackenzie Swaim
Harrisburg, Pennsylvania

Insomnia

I am very much amused,
At what they say you do,
If you have insomnia,
So I will tell it all to you.
Eat an onion
Before you retire.
Warm your feet
Before an open fire.
Eat a banana,
Sip a spoonful of honey,
Quit worrying about everything,
Especially your money.
Drink some warm milk.
Count the everlasting sheep,
Learn to relax
And Sleep, Sleep, Sleep.
If you try all of these
It will soon be light,
If you could not get to sleep now,
You will tomorrow night.

Esther Mennen
Truman, Minnesota

Haiku

Bruises wash away
While my dreams dance on the beach
Solving tomorrow.

Mildred Hope Wood
Cedar Falls, Iowa

Haiku

We all have to go
and when my time comes
I hope I'll go through a forest.

Esther Edleman
Lost Nation

Artillery

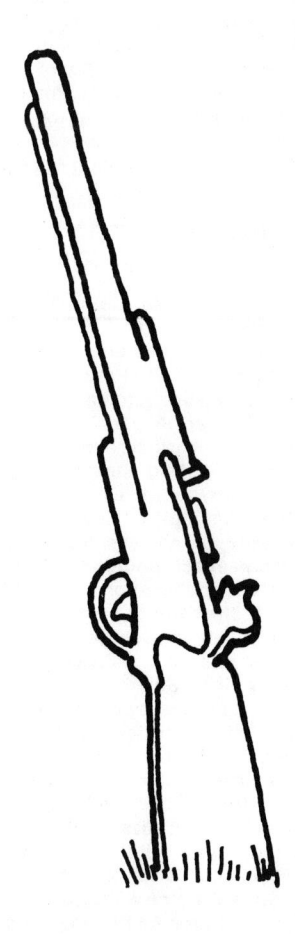

JIM ALBRIGHT is a Church of the Brethren pastor in Bryan, Ohio. He finds inspiration for his poetry in his encounters with the "number of things" that "the world is full of," and in the hurts and hopes of the people he meets in his work. . . . **ARTHUR C. FRICK** is a painter and professor of art at Wartburg College in Waverly, Iowa. . . . **FRANCES CONKLIN FRENCH,** mother of 6 and grandmother of 10, likes to swim and golf. She writes plays, essays and poetry; creative stitchery is also a hobby. She has won 2 state & 3 national DAR honors in in music, drama, art and creative stitchery. . . . **WILL C. JUMPER,** professor of English at Iowa State University in Ames, was in the U.S. Navy during World War II — and has numerous area ribbons, battle stars and a medal to prove the fact. . . . **MICHAEL G. KELLY's** biography appears in Chapter 3. . . . **JANET MADISON,** 29, is a newspaper journalist and free-lance writer. She has been writing poetry since adolescence and has had several pieces published. . . . **JOSEPH H. OATES,** 27, is a laborer and part-time student. He has been writing for only two years and has already been published in 3 other anthologies. . . . **MELVIN F. STEPHENS,** M.F.S., is a college grad who majored in English and poetry. He saw combat in Korea and earned 7 medals. He has won numerous awards for his prose and poetry. . . . **CURT L. SYTSMA,** a Des Moines attorney, is a nationally syndicated columnist who comments in verse on political and social issues. He is the author of a book, *The Rhyme & Reason of Curt Sytsma,* recently published by CSS Publications. . . . **GLENDA WINDERS,** on leave from a doctoral program at the University of Missouri, currently teaches at Central Missouri State University. Her short stories and essays have appeared in *Mandala, The Thornleigh Review,* the Kansas City *Star,* and *Midlands.* . . .

Love Does That
Continued from page 104...

female relationships. Besides writing, Sheila enjoys cross-country skiing, traveling & collecting old furniture. . . . **MIKE PAUL,** 37, ex-English teacher, is now editor of a newsletter for a car rental agency. He's planning a line of original greeting cards with his friend & writing partner, Charles Hupfer, who will do the art work. A romantic, Mike calls his poems "word pictures." . . . **ROB ROSS,** 32, is an art teacher and has written forever. He considers poetry another form of artistic expression — taking the raw material of thousands of words and "painting" them in a way that no one done before. . . . **THOM ROSS,** 29, follows coyote while hunting and paints lost polar explorers. Late at night Billy the Kid supplies the wine and for 5 years Jackson, Wyoming, has been home. "Hey, Sarah, let's float the Snake today." . . .**CHERYL SANDERS,** 28, enjoys horseback riding, dancing & writing. This is the first poem she has submitted for publication. . . .**PAMELA SNOW,** 34, is a composer, pianist, artist and poet. She likes to hike with her dog, Beth. . . . **L. J. SZUMYLO,** 20, is a Russian major at Georgetown University whose poetry serves her as an emotional release. . . . **JANE TERRANDO** is a wife, mother and nurse who enjoys writing. She has been published in several anthologies, and is completing her first book, *The Encounters of Life.* . . .**CAROL FOX THORNE** majored in English literature at Wheaton College. She has contributed to the *Prairie Light Review,* and recently had a hymn published . Walking and the piano are major interests, but poetry is her first love. . . .**GLENDA WINDERS,** on leave from a doctoral program at the university of Missouri, currently teaches at Central Missouri State University. Her short stories and essays have appeared in various publications. . . .**EVA S. WOOD,** 26, is an engineering technician at a Detroit television station. Favorite distractions include music and movies. A home video enthusiast and part-time photographer, she hopes someday to combine her poetry and photographs in a book.

Artillery

The roadside ditch
Along the bamboo grove
Conceals from sight the viscid rot
Of farmer's wives who died upon the place
Where gleaming crickets sang.

Okinawa

The ancient skulls
About the broken wombs
Of Buddhist graves at Itoman
Gaze sightlessly into the yellow haze
Around the newly slain.

The Perimeter

The sentinel
Sneaks by the field of cane
Alert to every rustling leaf
Which might reveal the stalking enemy
And abrupt searing death.

Oh, Lebanon

When twilight comes
And pine groves against the sky
Mantle the hills dark gold and blue,
And mountain lavender softly exhales —
My mind turns home again.

Arthur C. Frick
Waverly, Iowa

Out of the Cradle

For days
and nights and days
I've sought shelter
in these ruins;
Watching
from disintegrating sills
as militiamen hunt
everything they can kill;
Seeing signs in starless nights,
signs of directions in living
while they lie dying;
Listen . . .
I heard a child moan —
"Oh God please don't let them see me cry."

Janet Madison
Traverse City, Michigan

The Head Nurse & the Warrior

The Head Nurse spoke to me of love today.
She had had two dead husbands,
And was a new grandmother of two weeks.
She spoke to me today.
    I told her two dead husbands
    Did not equate three massacres
    In ten minutes
    On the battlefield.
She, single, spoke to me of love.
And, I, a young man, could not usher her in,
Tho I could see her point of view.
    O, Love,
    Where have you gone
    So fast,
    And so quick!

Melvin F. Stephens
Chicago, Illinois

Interview with a Veteran, 1980

So what does it matter? Eh? I'm deef, you know.
The guns, the Great War guns, they made me deef.
Speak up; don't mumble! Better. Sure, reporter,
I read your paper, have for umpteen years.
How old am I? Sonny, you make a guess.
Dead wrong! I'm eighty-three and holding —
    count down
like the astronauts! What's that? Artillery? Sure,
I fired the guns and groomed the horses. But
    trenches
weren't really the place for horses; we fought a war
by rules that's passed their usefulness, you know?
Draft? Yeah, I was drafted. Didn't have no kids
for "weatherstrips" against the draft, they used
to say. And now? Yeah, sure, I read your paper.
I'm old. I get confused with all your babble.
Sabres are rattling. Who is threatened by who?
We knew why we fought the Great War, and the
    next.
But what's the argument now? Oh lordy, lordy,
I'm tired. So 'scuse me; I gotta take a nap.

Will C. Jumper
Ames, Iowa

Roosevelt's Birthday

They talk about Roosevelt's birthday.
They can have him. I'll not celebrate
That man. Or his life.
Both my boys were in the war. My Jack,
They made him a paratrooper. They
Talked him up so. Said he had the perfect
Build for jumping. My boy.
They would drop them way behind the lines.
Then the boys must get back on their own.
Friends of his wrote in a letter how it
Happened. In Holland.
He knew. He told his buddies, You'll be back
Walking down this street again. Not me.
I said, Get out. But no.
William says, If they called me today
I wouldn't go. They took him out of school,
Put him in a tank.
They shot in front of him and all around.
Never hit his tank. They hit his rifle
Once. He kept the piece
Where the bullet hit. When it gets cold
The mark across his cheek turns white as death.
He wasn't meant to go,
I guess. I used to talk about my Jack
All the time until someone told me
I talked about it too much.
So I don't talk about Jack now. William
Says, I never aimed at anybody.
He'd be fifty-six.

Jim Albright
Bryan, Ohio

Taps

I have nothing but my bugle, sir,
But I'd like to blow the *Taps*
O'er the grave of that old soldier, sir,
The one who tossed his cap
Into the air when e'er the band
Went down the street
And Old Glory fluttered gallantly
To the drummer's quickened beat.
I have nothing but my bugle, sir,
But I'd like to face the East
And blow the final resting notes
O'er a life that's ceased.
"Day is done" and now he's found his peace,
If only it were true
Through all the west and east.
"Gone the sun" — though the sun is never gone,
It rises in the morning to
The bugler's testy song.
"Safely rest" — like the babe upon his bed,
I've nothing but my bugle, sir,
The blue, the white and red.

Frances Conklin French
Loves Park, Illinois

First Shot

Slowly,
the finger squeezes the trigger.
Suddenly —
the force
of many dead
and the sound
the cries of all fallen
soldiers and victims
pierce
the quiet of a fraction of before.

———

Slowly,
the instrument is lowered
protectively to the table.
While,
the target is brought back
to the hand that has bitten it.

———

With the feeling of a conqueror and victor —
a smile emerges on a troubled face.

Joseph H. Oates
Youngstown, Ohio

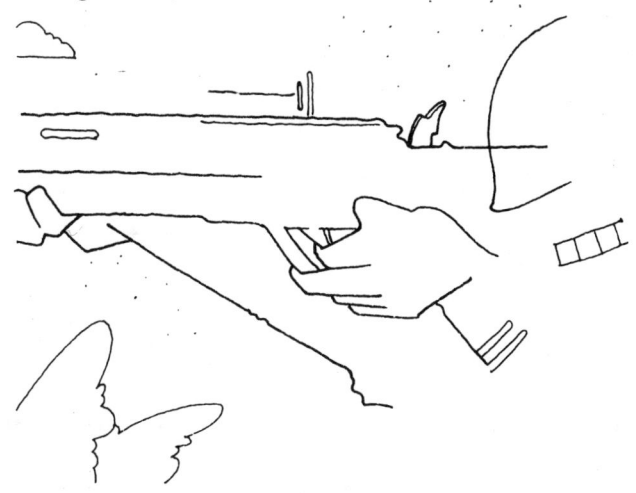

Middle West
(in protest of nuclear warfare)

Tired of the busy life in a big city,
I moved to the peaceful part,
Where women wear aprons,
And men driving pickup trucks
Wave at people they don't even know.

Where gaping black holes
Belch forth enough venom to kill us all,
And the wind howls
While lonely, frozen guards
Check to see if birds have landed on the barbed
  wire

It is quiet here.
In my porch swing I hum old songs and sip
  lemonade.
I dust lampshades
And pretend to ignore
The searchlight on the horizon.

Glenda Winders
Warrensburg, Missouri

Countdown

"Ten." The voice avoids emotion,
Science slicing silence through,
Digits droning toward commotion,
Crossing seas naively blue.
Ten is symbol of our science,
Cat we keep, but can't control,
Purring through the small appliance,
Scratching terror in our soul.

"Nine." The faceless intonations
Pierce the precious morning calm.
Nine, the number of the nations
Who have built the blasted bomb.
Every year, another finger
Hovers near another switch;
Sometimes fingers learn to linger.
Sometimes fingers start to itch.

"Eight." The voice continues counting,
Droning digits down because
Other numbers have been mounting;
Numbers bow to backward laws.
Eight is symbol of the atom,
Circled forces strong as doubt.
First, we found them in the atom;
Then we had to let them out.

"Seven." Strange, the spoken number
Lost its lustrous, sacred spell.
Soldiers march as leaders lumber;
Numbers drone their way toward hell.
Seven seas and seven sages —
Seven ways to make a buck.
Saints and sinners lose their wages;
Lucky seven lost its luck.

"Six." The voice is paced and certain,
Far removed from what will be.
Who will draw the bedroom curtain
When the atom wanders free?
Six, the day in one lost August,
Nineteen hundred forty-five;
Heat beyond the heat of August
Burned a city's souls alive.

"Five." The voice avoids emotion.
Science slicing silence through.
Why does sunlight kiss the ocean?
Why are morning skies so blue?
Five is strange, somehow unfinished;
Five describes the state of men —
Still alive, but so diminished,
Haunted half of what has been.

"Four." The sound is sin's annointing,
Verbal vomit, faceless mouth.
Is it true the bombs are pointing
East and West and North and South?
Four is symbol of the corners
Of our world that have the bomb.
Will that world have room for mourners
When the atoms break the calm?

"Three." The holy sound pre-empted —
Father, Son and Holy Ghost.
Will the churches be exempted
When the nations start to roast?
What was wrong with all our learning?
Why, in love, did we persist
Spreading means of instant burning?
Did we choose to not exist?

"Two." The graceless intonations
Sear the ear like Satan's cuss.
Did we own our own creations?

Did they not in fact own us?
Two is peace and combination;
Marriage, business, hope take two.
Did we join to save creation?
Did we pay the bomb its due?

"One." The all so near to zero
Sounds the essence of our soul.
Will there, could there, be a hero
When the atoms take control?
Countless blameless children slumber,
Dreaming dreams of mom and dad.
One is such a lonely number. . . .

Curt L. Sytsma
Des Moines, Iowa

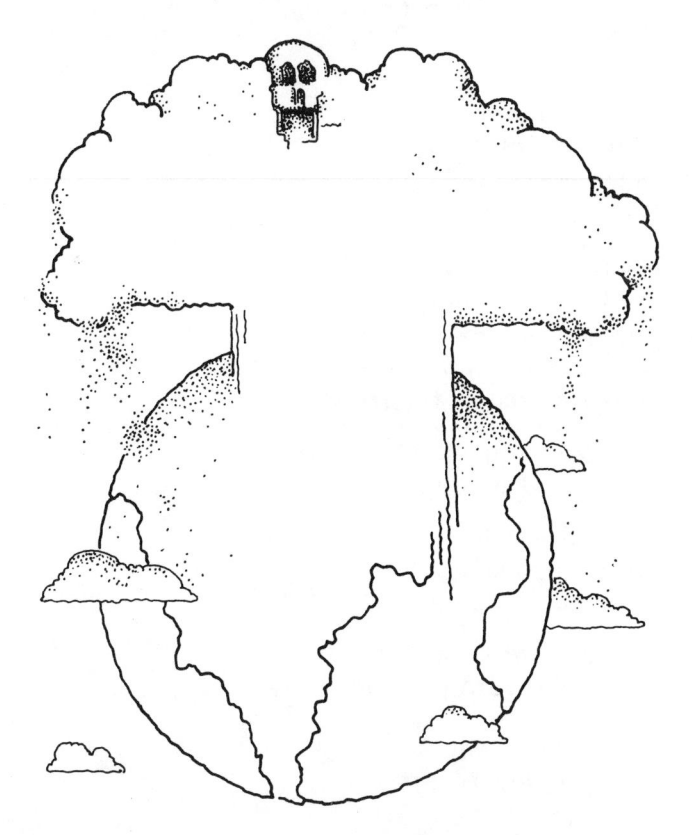

Lessons Learned by Survivors

Sign on the wall at a gathering of Holocaust survivors in Jerusalem, 1981:
> "Anyone who was at Mauthausen in the year 1942 and knew my brother Alexander Kopelmann, please, please contact me!"

The world doesn't
know how to mourn
you, Alexander.

We live in a place
you wouldn't comprehend.
A brother has bridged
your time and ours.

Sometimes he understands
sometimes he doesn't.
But he is still searching.

His note on the wall
says he is hoping
to touch you again
in some tattered
reminiscence of a
look, a word,
some fragment of
the mind's photography;
just a crumb of
conscious, human contact
with your days of horror.

I suspect you want to know
what we've learned since Mauthausen.

All I can say is that
the Holocaust continues . . .
more subtle to be sure.

One day, when we learn how,
we shall mourn you Alexander.

Michael G. Kelly
Apple Valley, Minnesota

Tomorrow's Rain

GAIL LYNN DANE, 16, is a junior at Kokomo High School. She has been writing poetry for 2 years and someday would like to publish a complete book of poems. This is her first published poem. . . . **MICHAEL F. FELSBURG,** 9, is a third grader at Platte River Elementary School. He enjoys writing and drawing in his free time. Flyfishing, bike riding and swimming are his hobbies. . . . **TARA LYNN HERRINGA,** 11, lives in the little Village of Lake Ann in Northern Michigan where she enjoys swimming, farming and singing. She attends Benzie Central Junior High. Her future goals include cross country running, raising horses, and someday teaching elementary school. . . . **EARTHA MELZER,** 8, has been writing poems and stories since she was 5. She recently co-authored a collection of poems, *Rainbow Patterns,* which was privately published last year. Eartha enjoys dancing, singing and travel. . . . **EMILY ROSE,** 12, a seventh grader at Washington Junior High, Dubuque, participates in chorus, plays the flute, and is a member of the Youth Ballet Company. Her poem, "The Wind," appeared in *Moments in Time* in 1980 and "The Face" was her contribution to *Images of Our Lives* in 1981. . . . **ANDREW ROBERT SCHUHLER,** 9, is a fourth grade student at Platte River Elementary. He enjoys art, BMX racing and Cub Scouts. This is his first published poem, due to the encouragement of Mrs. Szymanski, his third grade teacher. . . . **JENNIFER ANNE SIMPSON,** 11, was born in London, Ontario, and was encouraged in her writing by teachers at Arthur Ford Public School. She has been writing poetry for 5 years. She currently resides in Joplin, Missouri, and attends Lafayette School. Her hobbies are reading, writing and family travel. . . . **ERIKA THOMAS,** 14, has been writing poetry since the age of 7. She is entering her freshman year at Shadle Park High School and aspires to be a well-educated professional person. "Love" is her first published poem. . . . **ANGELA VYVERBERG,** 11, is a sixth grader at East Side Elementary School of Decorah. The daughter of Jere and Mary Vyverberg, she has a 9-year-old sister, Amanda. Angie began writing poetry one year ago; she also enjoys reading and drama. . . . **BECKI WITTE,** 14, a high school freshman, finds poetry and piano playing an emotional outlet. Becki is a staff member of her high school paper. She has enjoyed both reading and writing poetry for two years.

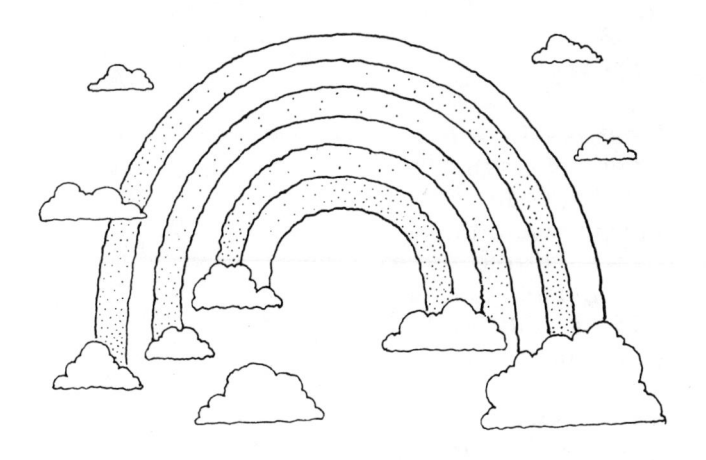

Tomorrow's Rain

The rainbows
    will be ours,
        until
Tomorrow's rain
    washes them away.

Emily Rose
Dubuque, Iowa
Age 12

Winter

With the white scattered snow
In the middle of the forest,
Near an old oak tree, lies
The frozen water. On
Each side of the water there are
Rows of thick ice; too cold to touch.

Gail Dane
Kokomo, Indiana
Age 16

Victory

I feel like the winter sunset
when I'm victorious.
I spill my colors over
the snow and the sky,
I am so terrific and exciting.
I am blushing red and bold blue.
I am beautiful and
everyone loves me!

Eartha Sarah Melzer
Interlochen, Michigan
Age 8

Love

He stood sullen
In the dull and dreary
silence of the downpour
A drawn face, obviously
a man of many problems
You could see it in
his eyes, it was written
in the lines on his face
What he was beginning
to die for, was what had
already died
It was taken from him
so abruptly, stolen by an
innocent person
                    Love

Erika Thomas
Spokane, Washington
Age 14

The Snowstorm in Me

A snowstorm spreads its
icy wings
and blows
its freezing breath,
down on the high,
snowy banks
that it had already left.

When someone tries
to manipulate me,
I become as furious
as that snowstorm.
I scream and rage in frustration,
and then become calm and still.

Tara Lynn Herringa
Lake Ann, Michigan
Age 11

One Track Mind

I'm like the winter wind
because I'm swift and quick.
When somebody disagrees with me,
I'm likely to be rough
With them.
I blow and blow,
I'm gloomy, icy, gray, vain.
I have a one track mind.

Michael F. Felsburg
Honor, Michigan
Age 9

Feelings in Flight

When I am happy
I feel like a falcon
soaring through the sky —
over the icy mountains
and over the countryside.

When I am mad
I am like Space Ship Columbia —
flying swiftly through
the universe
like a furious star.

Andrew Robert Schuhler
Lake Ann, Michigan
Age 9

Fog

Fog is as bad as a hog.
It makes me feel
   like a bump on a log.
Though it makes your skin nice,
It's like watermelon and rice.
It just doesn't go together
   with ME!

Jennifer Simpson
Joplin, Missouri
Age 11

My Thoughts and Dreams

I dream of a beautiful place
Where the water runs pure and blue
and as I walk through the tall grass
I am thinking of you.

I think of what a beautiful place
this world could really be
and what a wonderful time I'd have
if you would walk with me.

I dream of a grassy meadow
with the smell of flowers so sweet
but without you walking with me
My world is not yet complete.

Becki Witte
Lost Nation, Iowa
Age 14

Together (Friends)

Walking through the woods
On an early summer morn,
Watching all the squirrels tumble
While a baby bird is born.

Singing in the concert
Or soaking up the sun,
We are always together
And we're always having fun.

Doing all our homework
And spending all our money,
Eating bread and butter
And eating toast with honey.

Always walking to school,
Always riding our bikes,
We'll be together at our camp
And we'll be partners on the hike.

We'll go shopping tomorrow
And we'll go together, of course.
We'll go walking all around
Then we'll ride my horse.

Angela Vyverberg
Decorah, Iowa

**Love
Does
That**

TINA ABOLINS, 20, is a commercial art major at Grand View. She writes about experiences in her life; poems are her personal autobiography.... **RONALD L. "ANDY" ANDRZEJEWSKI,** insurance agent and Dale Carnegie course instructor, has been writing for personal pleasure for 20 years. This is his first attempt at being published.... **J. KARYL ARNOLD's** bio sketch appears in Chapter 4.... **KATHLEEN O'BRIEN DAVIN,** 26, has been writing poetry for 4 years and would like to develop a career in writing. This is her second appearance in a CSS Publications anthology. She is also interested in art and music.... **NOLA DEFFENBAUGH,** mother of 4, has always been interested in emotions, and has used writing via diaries and journals as a means of defining or expressing her own feelings, thoughts and observations. She seldom submits material, but the theme "human emotions" of the CSS Publications contest prompted her to enter.... **MARGERY DISBURG,** widow, church secretary, mother and grandmother, dearly loves family and friends, reading and writing, and being published the second year here.... **BRIAN FINNEY,** 24, majored in English at North Dakota State University. He now lives on a farm in northern Minnesota.... **CARL EARLY GILLESPIE, JR.,** is an avid potter and a native of Independence, Missouri. He composes in the early dawn hours....

JANE GRIGGS, mother of 6 and grandmother of 3, is very active in St. Paul's Lutheran Church of McClure, Ohio. "I have many hobbies, and always carry a tablet, just in case a thought for a poem comes to me. Someday I would like to write a novel."... **MILA GUDDING,** 47, is the mother of 4 children and has 3 grandchildren. She likes to play the piano, paint and draw and refinish furniture. She has been writing poetry for about 25 years and hopes to write a book someday. This is her first published poem.... **GEORGIANN D. HAGEN,** 24, is an English teacher at the junior high in Rock Falls, Illinois. She enjoys writing poetry while listening to music in the solitude of the late evening hours. ... **JILL HAMILTON,** 22, enjoys writing in her spare time; she also enjoys photography and being outdoors. She is awaiting the arrival of her first child... . **SHARON HARRIS,** 30, is head bookkeeper and computer operator at Citizens National Bank of Park Rapids, Minnesota, and has worked there for 14 years. She has been writing poetry for 15-20 years and has 15 poems published in the last few years.... **BRENDA R. JOHNSON,** 25, has had several poems published while in high school and attributes her new-found inspiration to country music singer Helen Cornelius, whose encouragement has prompted her to consider publishing a personal anthology of her poems.

MELLENIA DeCOTEAU JONES, a rambunctious Arien, was born and reared in Savannah, Georgia, and moved to Washington, D.C., in late 1975. A capable lyricist and songwriter, her first book of poetry will be published soon.... The bio sketch of **MICHAEL G. KELLY** appears in Chapter 4.... **ELEANOR M. KERR,** former teacher of English & journalism in high school and college, is busy with community, family & business activities. Writing skits and poetry is a part-time hobby.... The bio for **JUDY KEYSER** is given in Chapter 2.... **MARK LAWSON,** 20, has been writing poetry & short stories for 5 years. He also plays saxophone & drums, and is currently co-forming a 60's pop band. Mark hopes to have a collection of stories & poems published in the future.... **NANCY BRIER O'NEAL,** 36, mother of 2 daughters, is presently employed by the Texas department of public safety. She has been writing poetry for 3 years, having had about 50 poems published nationally in various magazines, anthologies, newspapers and quarterlies.... **SHEILA JOY PACKA** is a social worker and a feminist living in northern Minnesota. Much of her writing explores male/

Continued on page 82...

Love Does That

When your sun shines
and the sun isn't up.
When you smell the flowers
and they're not in bloom.
When raindrops glisten
falling through the air,
and your day seems bright
when it's full of gloom.
When someone you love
makes you want to laugh.
When you open your eyes
and you want to smile.
What a glorious feeling,
Enjoy it my friend.
Love does that
Once in a while.

Jane Griggs
McClure, Ohio

Giggles in the Wind

You make me laugh!
Like a child caught up in freedom,
I giggle in the wind and
catch an elusive memory of
happiness
In the space between then and tomorrow
I love
the way you make me laugh!

Cheryl Sanders
Terre Haute, Indiana

Dear Friend

Tomorrow when I see you,
And you raise your eyebrows in greeting;
While we sharpen our tongues
In a word duel
Over a bowl of soup at Stones,
I will laugh
For the first time that day,
And for a few minutes,
Watching your beard
Camouflage the elaborate nonsense
Emoting therein,
I will forget the boredom of a job
And agree with you
That, basically,
The world is corrupt,
And we should mount our camels
And flee.

Margery Disburg
Marshalltown, Iowa

Upon Visiting an Old Friend

Like a well-worn coat
your life fits you.
In it you move
easily:
Hanging your children's clothes
in rows
(neatly pressed and mended).
Scrubbing your floors
once a month.
Mailing birthday and anniversary cards
precisely two days ahead.
You are comfortable,
easy.

Why does my coat
tug and pull
in all the wrong places?
Sometimes I want to rip it off,
throw it away —
so that I can learn whether,
without it,
I would be
Free.

Carol Fox Thorne
Wheaton, Illinois

She and I

Crossing over to the other side;
I step forward, and in she glides.
Without a second's notice;
No warning or no alarm,
She stops at nothing until she reaches your arms.
Pretending all the time not to really care,
But putting aside all the things until she's right
    there
Laughing, talking, loving, giving . . .
    mm-mm-mmmph.
The soul has melted and I'm back to me.
Feeling good, though ashamed and somewhat
    guilty.
Wanting to change the past to make it be,
A beautiful moment in my life's history.

Crossing back into reality, as a matter of fact;
She hesitates, but I snap her back into the act.
Calming her down,
Cooling her out, erasing the pain;
A love once shared will soon come again.
Just go on pretending not to really care,
Yet deep down inside wanting to be there to share;
A smile, a laugh, a word, a touch,
A feeling of wholeness which I need so much.
Dreaming of it gives my spirit a rush.
Waking, . . . then fantasizing once more about us,
One tear falls as my thirst to quench my desires
    are hushed.

E. Mellenia DeCoteau Jones
Washington, D.C.

A Step Behind

God, I'm tired.
Too many miles, so many foreign lands.
How many season changes spent
searching for love,
always a step behind.

Love's not in Rome
regardless what the Pope says.
Nor in Spain, Mr. Hemmingway,
and Philadelphia is a farce.

Often I've heard it voiced
on bar stools,
in back seats,
between silk sheets,
con jobs for hot pants.

I've walked where it's been —
In green fields after rain,
on glistening beaches
earlier kissed by waves,
in tearful eyes of ex-virgins,
me, always a step behind.

i've sensed its wondrous workings
in empty birds' nests,
in knowing smiles on aged corpses,
on ladybugs released from children's mason jars,
me, always a step behind.

Perhaps I've searched wrong places
with eyes too blind to see.
I think I'll rest atop a hill
and let love catch up to me.

Ronald L. Andrzejewski
Belmont, Michigan

Waiting

I have sat in this window and waited for years.
I've watched for a red Porsche, a silver Mustang,
A pick-up truck with Oklahoma license plates.
I've waited for lovers who came
And some who didn't,
Seen headlights bounce off the fronts of houses
And played games like
"His will be the third car"—
Or the eighth, or the fifteenth.
I've run from this chair to the bathroom,
Combed my hair and glossed my lips,
Dialed time and temperature
To make sure my watch hadn't stopped,
Put a log on the fire
And had one glass of wine
For courage.

Today I bought curtains for this window.
Heavy blue drapes that close over drawn shades,
Satin and tapestry
That keep headlights and loneliness outside,
And inside I am protected
From waiting.

Glenda Winders
Warrensburg, Missouri

To a Marble Statue
In a Public Park

Marble maid with unlined brow,
I envy you your calm, and how
You watch the crowds with languid poise
Indifferent to pain and joys;
While with anxious eyes I scan
The passing throng for one tall man.
    He said he'd meet me here at four —
    It's thirty minutes past or more
And still he does not come. To you
With granite heart, what men may do
Will never cause concern; to me
It matters quite a lot, you see.
Perhaps I too should cultivate
A high disdain for man — But wait,
Is that he on that distant bench?
Then keep your calm, stone-hearted wench,
Your cold perfection men admire —
Warm, human *love* I would inspire!

Eleanor M. Kerr
Coats, Kansas

The Meeting

We were introduced
By a mutual friend
As to who I was
And who you were
We talked into
The night
Drinking our beer
Now we've shared
Good times and
A laughter to
Call our own
Cuz when you
Took my hand and
We walked barefoot
In the rain
I fell in love
With you
For now . . .
For ever . . .
For always

Jill Hamilton
Iowa Falls, Iowa

Take My Hand

I would walk along the sand
In perfect harmony with living
In a world of dreamy smiles
And
Warm happiness

I would feel the cool foamy feathers
Of the water
Splashing life into my somber body
And
Intoxicate my senses
With the tingling forcefulness

I would hear the songs of sea birds
In their daily search for existence
And
Laugh with their laughter
As the sun sprinkles colors on the
Fullness of their beauty

I would close my eyes
And allow myself to travel to this place
Only knowing
My hand could reach out and be accepted
In the loving security of your hand
And
My love returned gently by your love
And
My soul bound spiritually with yours

Kathie Jacquin
St. Louis, Missouri

About Dawes Park

I might take you
if you think you would
understand the place.
If you think you would
understand the waves
and rocks
If you think you would
know the people
and why.
I might take you
and I don't take everyone.
But you must sit
on cement benches
feeding squirrels from
your hand.
You must walk the path
back and forth
and clear around.
You must come here
before the sun comes up
and know the gulls
and swallows.
You must enjoy
the smell in the air
and go barefoot
in the hot sand.
If you think you can
manage all these things
I might take you.
There is one more thing
and most important,
you must understand
why I come here.

Judy Keyser
Des Moines, Iowa

See through Snowfall

The day was ours
Beautiful, clear and white
The time was now
And everything seemed right.

We walked through the diamonds
That covered the ground
The day was so fresh
Like the friendship we'd found.

And as we were talking
I swear I could see
The outside and inside
Of the man next to me.

Inside you there longs
Another man yet to be
One lonely and loving
You want me to see.

I think I did see you
The first time we met
You looked at me fondly
And you look that way yet.

If time treats us gently
And slowly we go
Each to the other
We will get to know.

Mila Gudding
Moorhead, Minnesota

Minor Revision
(for SJW)

rattle, rattle, rattle,
two bullets in the skull rollin' round like
two dice that you
hold your hands over the eye holes so they don't
fall out.
release of the fingers and they drop onto the
    mahogany top
of the bar —— snake eyes ——
next to the whiskey glass.
a room full of people you don't know
and don't really care about. (low hushed murmur
    of the crowd.)
a tip of the hand to the bartender
the rattle of the keys to the truck and the sound
    of the bullets in the skull.

(hear hear the measured motion of the river as it
    winds forever
towards the distant sea.)
well, tonight the beer is cold
and the red wine is nice.
somewhere a cowboy goes out to die, alone,
under a sky
pregnant with rain clouds. much like the kind that
    inhabit
montana and this part of wyoming in the summer.
high with summer heat and rain.
shadows stain the mountains and the rain settles
    the dust.
it is like living where a new baby is born every day.
up the valley, to the north, the clouds hang over
    yellowstone
in blues and pinks.

a gin and tonic to the lips of a forgotten tourist.
here we drink beer all night and
piss under the constellations.
urine for a river.

walking along this road tonight in the
   approaching darkness
i heard a flight of
goldeneyes
overhead. their whistling wings in this faint light
   and i can not
make them out against the winter sky.
(under Orion truth is a lone stalk up a frozen river
the banks high with recent snow fall.
coyote tracks betray the presence of a previous
   hunter.
o, coyote — coyote — coyote
eyes of the magician,
cunning of the sun and the shadows that define
nothing.)
your measured breathing will comfort me tonight
and sleep descends like the fading sounds of the
   distant
wings of the goldeneyes
as they move north to reaffirm their love.

Thom Ross
Jackson, Wyoming

Sometimes: A Sestina

Sometimes
he stroked my hair with his hands
and watched my face
and listened unobtrusively to learn
I don't know what
about me.

What he wanted escaped me
although I wondered, sometimes,
behind the smoke of a lit cigarette, what
made him talk with his hands
like a deaf-mute. I could learn,
I suppose, to avoid his steady face.

It was this lack that he couldn't face
he blamed it upon me —
said it was I who would not learn
to be receptive and kind sometimes.
But I was afraid of his hands
and what they knew, somewhat.

He never left alone what
was mine and he tore pieces from my face
to keep on his own. His hands
kept coming to move me
toward him. Their pressure sometimes
felt like burns. He said I would learn.

He felt that if I could learn
to trace his finger along my breast, what
was left unsaid was better. Sometimes
I felt he asked too much and my face
blushed dark despite me
being in the shadow of his hands.

He touched me with his hands
then and stroked me. He would learn
what rhythm stilled me
and left what
was unsaid. My face.
turned away and I whispered, sometimes.

Until his unruly hands found my face
that could sometimes reveal what
I would not learn to say about me.

Sheila Joy Packa
Chisholm, Minnesota

Sierra Dawn

A flock of great grey geese
arises from a mist
and with an occasional barely audible honk
at random intervals
wheel, rapid, wild, and lonely.
Sounding, faster and faster, gathering, gathering
and with a mighty shout
as of thousands, and a thunder of wings
they fly right through my body.
My heart hammers, sobs, and stops. I take in a
    great breath and
shout in exultation.
In the satisfied darkness
two lovers kiss an end to the flight.

Carl E. Gillespie, Jr.
Independence, Missouri

1,2,U

The Flash of a Lash:

I once wrote about your eyes.
But you blinked
And washed the words away.
The funny thing is
If it would have been
Just one lid,
It would have been
A wink
Instead of
A lash.

Guilt:

Why is it
That upon entering
A court of law
I am innocent
   (please refrain from snickering)
Until proven guilty,
But when I walk into
A room filled with new faces,
All strangers — just like jurors,
I am guilty
Until approved?

We One (for j.a.):

Though it probably sounds profound
Or even silly
Or even stupid . . .

. . . I have often thought of you . . .
. . . As me . . .

But at the same time
I am both of us . . .
. . . And you are all that we'll ever be.

Mark Lawson
Fort Wayne, Indiana

Smiling

ah, my friend,
the others see me smiling at my work.
but it's not my work I'm enjoying.

all day long,
I keep getting flashes of you —
I see your hand reaching for me,
I have a quick memory
    of your face so close,
a brief glimpse of your lips opening
    to touch mine . . .

ah, I smile at my work. . .

Sharon Harris
Menahga, Minnesota

Dove

I want to
Soothe the pain that you
Hold.
I am powerless, maybe, to soothe
You, yet in
Time, you will be happy. I want, at
Times, to call you my sweet angel, but you'd
Laugh in mockery, and I, in my
Smallness and greatness,
Seek your approval.
The remnants of a February
Full moon
Shines on you, ethereal angel;
Your feathers pure and new close in
Sleep, and your absence, from me,
Leave unprotected,
Wild dreams.

Kathleen O'Brien Davin
Warren, Ohio

Performing Bear

I don't feel like being a performing bear today.
I hope you'll understand.
Today is a day for hibernating,
For giving in to my animal nature
By withdrawal from the world
To nurse my hurts in private and thus heal myself
Away from the cold fire of your prying eyes,
Your probing words and bustling, tidying actions
That try to dismiss my bad feelings
With a pat on the head or a sweep-under-the-rug.
Perhaps tomorrow will be a warm, sunlit day,
And you can poke me and prod me
While you exclaim how soft I am, what a gentle
    giant,
Denying the beast inside me
Because you don't want to see it.
I in turn will stand up tall and turn circles for you;
Perhaps even take you for a ride
Or hop on one foot to make you laugh,
Gratifying your every whimsical pleasure.
But tomorrow is not here,
And today stretches yawning with no stimulation.
Still, I will not be your performing bear just now.

J. Karyl Arnold
Medina, Ohio

Friendship

Sometimes after one of our arguments,
   I feel like hanging a "Going Out of Business"
     sign on our friendship
But then —
   I decide an "Out to Lunch — Back in an Hour"
     will do instead.

Mike Paul
Ft. Lauderdale, Florida

Love Gone Awry

You stare at me
with hungry eyes,
begging me to understand;
I don't.
You've raped my soul,
leaving me empty,
afraid,
and alone.
Walk away
before I strike at you,
furious with rage,
seething with hate.
You've taken from me
all I can give;
still you want more . . .
All I feel for you now
is pity,
pity,
because you don't understand
that love is a gift,
given freely,
not an expected reward.

Georgiann Hagen
Rock Falls, Illinois.

Crushed Petals

So untimely appeared the uneaten meal,
So excessively volumed seemed your nonchalant
    nibbling,
So smothering yet the blanket of silence
That I choked and fled — in that moment, unfitting.

So harsh was the sound of my name,
So weakly I answered you with "what?",
So hard was the anger glared out from your eyes
That I cried, deeply withheld, inside.

So wasted were flowers tossed out to the wind,
So bruised were their petals aground,
So crashing the blast of the broken vase
That I shook at the thundering sound.

Then so quietly you whispered "I need you",
And so loudly it echoed within,
So willingly was my vanity swallowed
As love's petals overgrew anger again.

Nancy Brier O'Neal
Cuero, Texas

Spring Thaw

The doorhinge creaks:
I sense your presence
although
my back is turned.

There's a pause:
Two hearts — hesitating.

I turn. Above the strained silence
of the barren winter our eyes meet.

You reach out
offering the first daffodil

Our hands touch and detect
the marvel of a melting point.

Doris T. Brokaw
Canton, Missouri

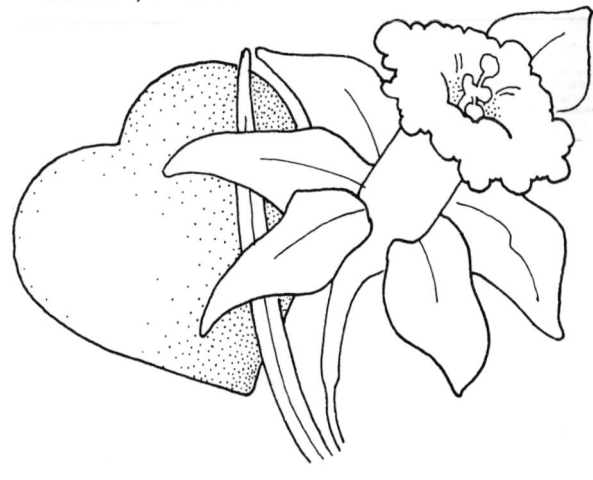

Distances

It doesn't seem impossible —
(just highly unlikely),
that there ever was a time
when I could put my hand out
and find you standing there,
within reach . . . .
Close enough to keep me from falling,
yet far enough so I still
breathe my own life.
Living within your grasp,
but staying without your love.
Needing you anyway,
because that's what you wanted. . . .
Loving you too much,
because that's what I wanted.
Held together by needs and wants
so very different,
and yet —
so much the same . . .
as we are the same.

Eva S. Wood
Inkster, Michigan

Checkmate

   I crawl
      underneath a compromise
and hide behind
a locked door.
   Quiet desperation
       prevails
in solitude
— even though you are
      beside me . . .

   Where does it end?
   When does the carousel
   stop spinning round
so I can touch ground?

   I slip
     into destiny,
silent despair
dwells within.
   Inside out,
     I claw
at a wall,
hoping to reach
      for a dream
        and become a reality . . .

   Will it ever end?
   Will this merry-go-round
   love keep spinning
til I faint and fall off
a horse?
   You are not my knight,
You are just a pawn
      that stands in my way.
   You are a man
— I cannot love.
Why won't you set me free?

Tina Abolins
Des Moines, Iowa

Rupture

Crises tear us;
our dialogue becomes
a torrent-fractured bridge.

Someday, someday
the heavy rains will cease.

Pamela Snow
Everett, Washington

The Blades

There
is hope
that
love
remains beneath
the
hate
and that
time may soothe
the
wounds.

The pain
may linger
while
sorrow fades
but
I'll
not escape
the
blades.

Rob Ross
Muncie, Indiana

Madness of No Method

You remember the madness
That came when love left
You shattered
And flailing
In a swirling sea

And now this new love
Presents itself
And you want to capsulize
Every moment
Every sound
Every smell
Every word
And place them under your tongue
As food for your dreams

But this new love
Contains the key
For that black box
Of memories
You have hidden in the dark
Recesses in your heart
And as the lid of that box
Rises
Slowly
Incessantly
All the pills in the world
Cannot restrain
That madness of no method

Brian Finney
St. Vincent, Minnesota

Watercolor

My mind controls the brushes
On the canvas of my soul.
To paint in watercolors
The love my memory holds.
For the dreams have run together
And they will never be as clear
As the times when you were with me
And it's best, since you're not here,
That time has softened all the edges
And muted all the hues
For my love's a watercolor
Misty memory of you.

Brenda R. Johnson
Iowa Falls, Iowa

Forbidden

(For R.)

I saw your face
In a moment's dreaming:
Worn and aged;
Years from now;
The eyes grow dim
And the lines grow deep,
To cut the flesh upon your brow.

I closed my eyes
And the tears bled softly;
Salted grief for what will be.
But I did not cry
For the youth that withers;
I cried that you'd not
Grow old with me.

L.J. Szumylo
Barrington Hills, Illinois

Casualty

Sitting here a thousand miles
    and twenty years away from you
You suddenly explode inside my head
Scattering shrapnel-sharp memories everywhere.

Jagged pictures cut into my day
    Ripping open old wounds
I thought time had healed.

So here I sit
    With blood on both my hands
While you're off somewhere shining in the sun.

Mike Paul
Ft. Lauderdale, Florida

Missing You

I started missing you early this time,
Before you had left for the train;
I turned the clocks off so I wouldn't know
When you'd pulled out of my life again.

You said it wasn't my fault you were going,
And I shouldn't feel I'm to blame;
Something had changed — when I lay in your arms,
Somehow it wasn't the same.

I tried to write to you, thinking I'd catch
These questions before they dissolved;
Somehow the words just got caught in the pain,
And left me with nothing resolved.

You said a promise had broken your spirit,
And silence had broken your heart;
I tried to reach you, but just couldn't find
The square in our lives that said "start."

Eva S. Wood
Inkster, Michigan

Leavetaking

Trains should always be
on time,
or even a little early,
so haste would be the only thing
uppermost in both our minds.

We should always arrive
at the last moment,
flurried and breathless,
so words would be impossible.

Then there would be no need
at all
to stand and wait,
shifting luggage,
trying
trying
trying
to say goodbye.

Martha K. Graham
Macomb, Illinois

Nightmoth

dusty wings crisscross night air
lifting the veil of your sleep.

I don't suppose you want to kill
it. I answer no. the
liberatedwomanwifemistressmotherfriend
who lies beside me is still made uneasy
in the presence of unknown nightflight
not unlike the
littlegirl she once was.

but I dare not think
myselfmalesuperior.

the voice which authors my thoughts
reminds me of my secret and notsosecretfears.
the dilemma is
that I may not by definition
speak so fearlessly
of them . . .

. . . and once again dusty wings
crisscross nightair

Michael G. Kelly
Apple Valley, Minnesota

Honorable Mention

Life

Life, what happened to the plans we made?
    I was to marry a starry eyed dreamer
    Have a white picket fence around my house
    Be a mommy to a half a dozen kids.

Life, what happened to the plans we made?
    Relationships were to grow — not dissolve
    Promises kept — not broken
    Togetherness — not loneliness.

Life, what happened to the plans we made?
    I was to laugh — not cry
    Talk instead of scream
    Be asked not ordered

Life, what happened to the plans we made?
    I was to be loved!

Jane Terrando
Sugarland, Texas

Love's Resurrection

Love — who needs it?
    Heartache, pain anger, jealousy
Two people hurting and hating, when all they
    want is love.
    Fighting, cursing, quarreling, crying
Two antagonists opening up their deep wounds,
    spewing out venom.
    Sharing, listening, understanding, ministering
Two friends beginning to understand how each
    really feels.
    Forgiving, embracing, caring, loving
Two lovers freed at last of the weight of anger and
    resentment —
    Ready to love and live.
Love — who needs it?
    I do

Nola Deffenbaugh
Coffeyville, Kansas

Concentric Circles

PATRICIA L. ANDERSON returned, after 30 years, to the river town where she grew up to re-purchase her grandfather's home. "I plan to continue my interests in writing, jazz & classical music and to enjoy the growing process of my 2 granddaughters." . . . **MARILYN J. BARNES**, 35, has had over 50 poems published in the past year and has won many awards in various poetry contests. She teaches poetry & guitar classes and is currently working on her second novel. "Knowing my words touch others' lives makes writing all the more rewarding." . . . **EVELYN J. BOETTCHER** has been writing poetry for years and has been published in numerous "little" magazines and several anthologies. She has a group of haikus ready for publication in book form. . . .

ENID M. BENNETT, 82, likes to write about people she knows or hears about; she takes a fragment of a story and changes it and adds to it until she has a poem. "The best emotional poems are written in the first person, even though they happened to someone else." . . .

AGNES K. BOGARDUS, a retired mathematics teacher, has 4 sons and 11 grandchildren. Although she has written poems for many years for the pleasure of herself and friends, except for school newspapers, this is her first published poem. She loves to travel. . . . **ZELMA COOPER BOMAR,** mother of 2 sons, has 3 grandsons and 1 great-granddaughter. She has written poetry since high school days and has been published in 6 poetry anthologies. An artist, she hangs & sells her paintings in the hospital lobby. . . . **SUE ANNE BRIGGS,** 19, is an art major at Clarke College in Dubuque, Iowa, and a PFC in the Army Reserve Medical Field. She loves jogging, water and cross-country skiing, sketching, being with Iowa relatives & friends, walking the sandy beaches of Lake Michigan, and visiting her family in Muskegon, Michigan. . . .
JOAN MERRYMAN BURNS, mother of 4, native of Iowa, attended and later taught in a one-room rural school. She married and moved to Georgia 30 years ago. She is presently working on a book of memories of Iowa farm life. . . .

CHRISTINE CHRISTIAN is a former teacher turned restauranteur. "I write because ideas just bubble out all of the time and putting them on paper seems to clarify them. This special poem is for Debbie H., a special girl!" . . . . **MARY DUPONT** is a Louisiana-born Texas resident who has 4 children & 7 grandchildren. "I write poetry for the sheer joy of writing, and am a lover of words: their moods, symbolism, sounds, and rhythm and rhyme." . . . **T.R. FELICE** says, "I am 31 years old, a legal secretary, single, a Capricorn, a cat-lover and I have no hobbies except writing. I have been writing fiction and poetry since I was 9 and am presently working on a mystery novel. I am an inveterate, avid and addicted reader of everything from comic books to classics." . . .

LORI ANN FITTERLING, 26, recently moved to a farm and, between tending the garden & raising 2 little girls, finds little time to write, mostly about her family and her life. . . . **GARRETT W. FLOYD,** 35, has been writing since age 15; he is inspired daily and only writes what he feels or experiences. He loves life and thanks God for it. . . . **ROSEMARY FREEMAN,** writer & homemaker, has just published her first book, a novel with a setting in Guatemala for young people. She enjoys Bible teaching, creative crafts, drawing and grandmothering. . . . **JEANNETTE GARAFOLA,** 58, recently retired from a career of working with retarded adults, centers her life around her 9 children and 18 grandchildren. "I have only 10 poems at present. More *may* follow." . . . **LE ROY HECKMAN,** 72, father of 3 & grandfather of 4, has written well over 500 poems since retiring 6 years ago. He joined the R.S.V.P. and shares his poems with the residents of senior high rises, churches and nursing homes. . . . **PAT KING** has been teaching herself Spanish and intends to get college credit for it on a CLEP test. She wrote the poem in this book after a former Venezuelan
Continued on page 218. . . .

Concentric Circles
**(to my sister and brother
and their families in Minnesota)**

Drops of rain

      disrupt

the pond's tranquil surface.

Concentric circles

      explore

the waves and ripples

of each other's ever-expanding,

overlapping,

sometimes intimate circles.

William P. Riddle
Colfax, Iowa

My House

I love my house, it is not grand
But maybe you can understand
How much it means to me.
It is not new and here and there
It shows the need of much repair.
If I explain then you will see
Why it is so dear to me.
I saw it built each board and stone
But didn't know it would be my own.
It was a plan of Mother and Dad
Bungalows were then the fad.
Just to rent, is what they thought
Otherwise a vacant lot.
Now they're gone and I'm alone
And for a long time this has been my home.
It's chuck full of memories from wall to wall
Some I don't know, others I shall recall.
This dear little house where I abide
Throws its arms around me when I step inside.
And the door swings in, to all who come
My friends are most welcome, everyone.
As I have said . . . . it is not grand
Like many houses in our great land
But I'm thankful for a place of my own
Be it ever so humble
It's my home sweet home.

Nelle McCain
Independence, Missouri

In the Morning

My coffee steams
              a shimmer
   to the paned windows,   beyond

Gently as a hand
              would caress
   the leaves; they move all as one,   a patterned stream

Against the glass
              they spread
   covering my window with their wetness,   placid

Alone at home
              I am
   with simple priorities,   asking:

"Would anyone believe how happy I am?"

Kathy A. Olson
La Crosse, Wisconsin

Present with a Past

Touching the ring in my hand
triggered a memory...
a day so many years ago,
the tears flow gently —
I remember looking through a drop of sorrow
and watching as my mother removed
the beautiful band from her finger.
As she set the symbol of her existence
in its own private place,
I remember how beautiful they were together,
my parents and my memories.
Now they are mine,
as I touch my present with a past.

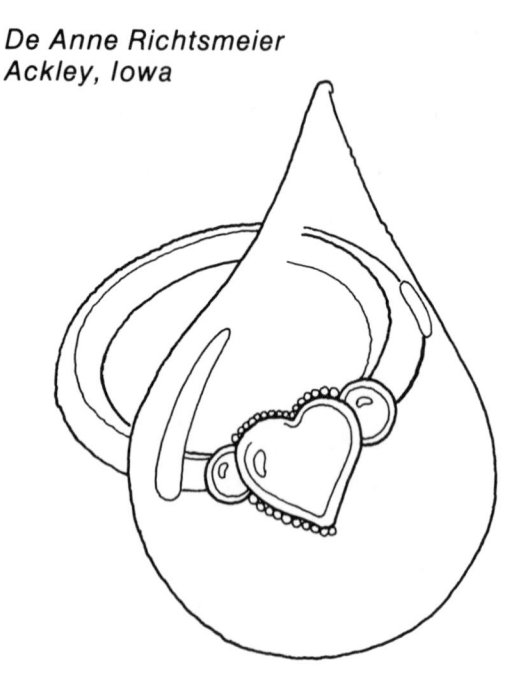

De Anne Richtsmeier
Ackley, Iowa

Cages

We share the morning kitchen, he in his wire cage
me at the cluttered counter, stirring up a cake.
The mixer whirrs a monotone accompaniment
to glorious trills which swell from his golden
   throat.
      How can he go on singing when for some
         reason
      God permits him not to fly?
      As birds must fly.
For myself, I abhor heights, but I dream of singing,
but am denied this talent by the Giver of all Talents.
I open the oven, smoothly slide the embryo cake in,
turn the timer to forty minutes. Crumbs from
   breakfast
and my careless baking litter the floor.
      My song is merely a sigh.
      As the electric broom begins its whirr
         the glory begins anew, trilling, beautifying
            kitchen
air in perfect unison with the wafting chocolate
   scent of
birthday cake. And with it comes the knowledge
that in our cages is strength, haven, and strangely,
   freedom.
      For God did not forget us.
      He lets us both do what we do best.

Dorthy M. Ross
Rochester, Illinois

Apples for the Oven

Sunday frequented our home
    with round green globes
    in robes of red,
Pippins preened for baking,
    cupped in mother's stubby hands,
    laid to rest in stainless steel,
The once firm center
    basking in the evening heat,
    becoming pablum-soft.

Never have I baked apples
    for my children's delight.
I entered that oven on every Sunday,
    my skin blistered to heated stones,
    my eyes encrusted with applesauce.
My children will never feel
    the pain of being cooked to perfection.

Marilyn J. Barnes
San Jose, California

Cold Turkey

The Christmas tree is still up
but I did not turn the lights on today.
The house is too quiet for lights.
Those last minutes are still rustling
through my mind like tissue paper:
    stuffing your suitcase with extra gifts
    wondering if the lock would hold
    wondering what would happen to me
    when you were ready to go
    and we finally looked at each other.
Today I threw out the last piece of fruit cake.
It was dry and stale.
I ate cold turkey and boiled cabbage for supper.
    Your eyes
    then your arms
    — and your beard —
    I had not supposed your beard would be
    so soft.
Through it all
I was all right
until later when I remembered
    seeing that you wanted to hug Dad too
    but you both fumbled a moment
    and then shook hands.

Pat King
Albia, Iowa

Honorable Mention

Parting with a Missionary Daughter

    Words . . .
Are there supposed to be words
    For such a time as this?
I cannot find them.
              If they do exist

Perhaps they lie
Locked in some secret passageway
    Of the soul
        Yes, that is it . . .

    Far away
I feel their small wings beating,
Beating . . .
But they are locked away,
    Sealed.
I cannot find the door
    Nor have I any key.

    Tears . . .
Surely there should be tears
    For such a time as this;
But I am smiling.
There are no tears.
            Or if there are
They cannot find their way,
Are prisoners in some subterranean channel
        Yes, that is it . . .

    Far away
I feel their small, hot fountain surging,
    Surging . . .
But they are locked away,
    Stopped.
The well is deep
    And I have nothing to draw with.

Others have words
   And tears,
But you and I
   Part with a quick embrace,
     A halting phrase.

O Daughter! Daughter!
   Godspeed . . .

Rosemary Freeman
Wichita, Kansas

Returned Embrace

Thank you, Mom and Dad
for teaching me
not just to keep the door open
when life is coming towards me . . .

    but to run out and meet it,
    to feel it when it embraces me
    and to give myself the courage
    to return its bravery

Constance Leigh Rentel
Tacoma, Washington

The Mother

Earthy she is, as the rich and fecund soil.
her laughter roles like thunder in low hills,
Her tears, the fall of refreshing rain.
The sharp edge of her Irish tongue
Cleaves through pretention to the bone of truth.
Her precepts, like the taste of wild bee honey,
Lie bitter on the tongue but turn sweet in the
 swallowing.
She shapes her children with her nurturing hands.
She breeds sons tall and straight as green corn
 growing.

Enid M. Bennett
Keokuk, Iowa

Mother

She would sit in the old green rocker
that dad bought her just after
they got married, with its torn casings
and worn arms, holding the book
of poems and at her feet my eyelids
would rise and fall in the cadence
of her voice. I grew to love it, her voice
with poetry beneath it.

I have to turn my head away as you
shake the tiny bottle of insulin
cold from the refrigerator, and measure
a precise amount into the needle and stick
yourself every morning while seated in
the old green rocker.

Dad asked me if there was anything
I wanted, after the funeral
I told him no, but he gave me the
rocker anyway. I've mended the
casings and refinished the wood,
and I pretend to hear your voice
rising and falling over the words
of the poets, as I read in the comfort
of the old green rocker.

Lori Fitterling
Lamoni, Iowa

A Mother's Prayer

Dear Lord, I pray that I may be
    Deserving of your trust in me.
You've placed a baby in my care,
    A tiny infant, sweet and fair.
His life I know depends on me,
    A grave responsibility.

I pray that I may teach him so
    That right from wrong he'll always know,
That kindness, justice, faith and love
    Will be his heritage from above.
That in all things, no matter where,
    He'll seek for daily help in prayer.

I pray that he will learn to see
    Beauty, in rain, the stars, a tree.
And hear, and understand when heard,
    The music in the song of a bird.
And know the pleasure that life brings
    In getting joy from simple things.

I pray that he will grow to be
    A man whom others, when they see,
Will trust at once, as hands extend,
    And want him for a valued friend.
So guide him, Lord, just all you can,
    This tiny babe, this future man.

Agnes K. Bogardus
Belvidere, Illinois

About Children

Rachel was five, with long blond hair tied up in
 braids that day.
Skin so white, looks translucent, like porcelain,
 I say!
Playing there on the lawn,
Reminded me of something — and then it was
 gone!

We talked a while, her mother and I, there on the
 porch, drank our tea.
I felt so content that summer day, with Rachel and
 her, so at ease!

She's begun to ask,
She's begun to ask me all sorts of things — it's
 hard, hard to answer, her mother said.
Like what? Well, for one, off the top of my head
 —who's God?!
And all I could think was (but I didn't say) — from
 my experience with children, that's not so odd.

We chatted on and I let it pass from mind, or so I
 thought —
Till next day it surfaced, up from my subconscious
 fought! I had begun to see!
That child is an angel, telling, not asking her
 mother (and me) —

To renew our search, to ask who's God?!
It's clear! Of course does not seem odd!
Are all little children God's angels, too — if only
 we'd listen, hear them speak —
would teach? Would teach?!

Betty C. Moore
Mt. Vernon, Iowa

A Treasure

Today I found a rock
in the pocket of my little boy's jeans,
and I felt both the sorrow and the joy
of a mother watching her baby
turn into a boy
of earthly treasures
and skyward dreams.
A little boy, just past two,
selected this water-smoothed rock
from the beach
and put it in his pocket —
a treasure.

Sally C. Medernach
Rockford, Illinois

Discovery

In spring he lies between us
singing his morning song.
His father murmurs, "my son"
a tug at my heart
I whisper softly, "ours"
afraid to lose this golden boy
to fishing, football, tug-a-war.
Hand on baby, one on mine
he says, "there is a joy in sharing."

Karen Murguia
Forest Park, Illinois

Branding

Late fall,
nudging into winter,
we covered the house
in the colors of the earth.
The boys took turns,
dressed in my old flannel,
arcing russet streaks
of their expression
over the faded yellow past;
while you, symbolic in farmer bibs,
stretched to the peak
on a ladder and a prayer
and laughed down
at my grounding fears.
We argued over detail,
and ended, for awhile,
with the east wall trim
half me,
half you,
collecting opinions . . .
Then finished by painting it "you,"
but the feeling was "us."

Becky Foght Melby
Union Grove, Wisconsin

My Children Are Made of Me

My children are made of me
   They cannot escape that.
It's too elementary to merely expound
   That my belly was their incubator.
My claim is more explicit.

I fixed the food that fed them
   I cut the cloth that clothed them
I bound the bruise that abased them
   I sang the song that soothed them
I levied the lesson that literated them
   I authored the advice that admonished them
I possessed the preconception that prejudiced them
   The sagacity of my wisdom swabbed them with acumen

My judgments, judged them
   My fears made them afraid
My endorsements became their endorsements.
   Gawd, it's awesome!

I was the initiator of their acknowledgment
   The cashier of their inheritance
The administrator of their charity
   I can never relinquish my dispensation
I am the recipient of their acceptance.

My children are made of me
   They cannot escape that
Nor can I.

Judy White
Jamestown, North Dakota

One

Only child . . .
One of a kind . . .
Sometimes . . .
I see a lonely look
In your eyes;
But the sky is great
And lovely.
The sun lays warm
Upon your face,
And everyone is lonely . . .
Sometimes.

*Patricia L. Anderson
Red Wing, Minnesota*

Hero Worship

I watched him grow
into the man
he is today;

Confident,
the metamorphosis
would come to pass.

Not with my hand
on the cradle
Or my heart, at his feet;

But like a child
at a bake-shop window,
nose pressed to the glass.

*Sandy Liska
Killingworth, Connecticut*

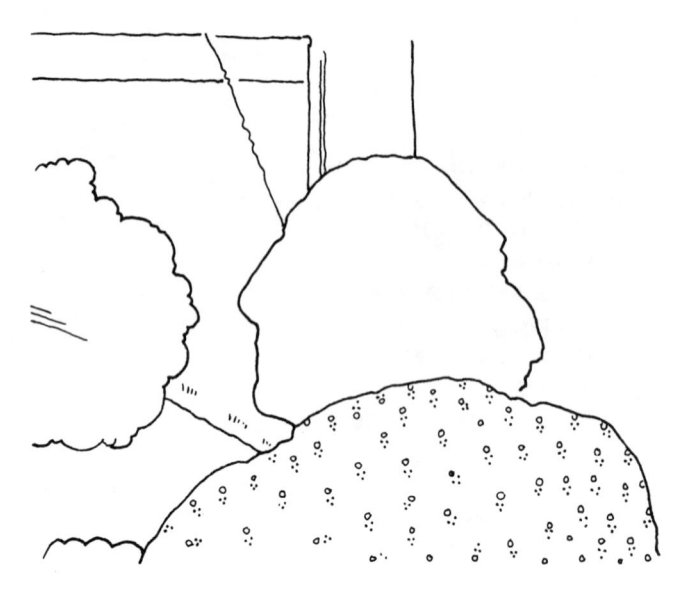

Answer

Staring out of aging windows,
Things look different
From this side of my eyes;
Questions remain half unanswered:
Who am I;
And why?

my boy rode away today;
Kicking up the dirt
He grew so fast;
Seemed he ripped
Right through his shirt.

I was a comfort to him,
And he a rock for me;
He is the answer
To what I could not be.

Garrett W. Floyd
Kokomo, Indiana

Grandson

The Grandson, with the touseled hair.
He was here yesterday —
And the day before.
Suddenly he is gone,
Out there, in strange places.
He was a little boy, trusting —
Wanting stories of "Alice in Wonderland"
Or making stars with toothpicks.
Now he has gone —
To far places.
The intimate memory remains,
Of stories shared and butterflies.
Knowing he must go,
Leaving footprints on my heart

Zelma Bomar
Cherokee, Iowa

Granddaughters

Dresden dolls.
Smokey lashes,
Golden curls,
Dimpled,
Grandma's girls,
Intent
On playing marbles

Grandsons

Impy, sunbrowned faces
Creep into heartsoft places,
Then dart away.

Jeannette Garafola
Ironton, Minnesota

A Belated Apology

"Show me how to catch a ball,"
I heard a young voice say.
I knew I should, but I would stall
And say, "Some other day."

"Dad, show me how to hit a ball.
You promised me you would."
But I'd say, "Son, you're still too small,
It won't do any good."

"Well, I know how to throw a ball.
Will you play catch with me?"
I caught a couple, I recall,
But with reluctancy.

Those memories haunt me now and then,
And it is well they should.
I'd like to have that chance again,
But wishing does no good.

I'd like to now apologize
For things I never did.
I was too dumb to realize
What those meant to a kid.

I sure am glad you aren't like me.
For no doubt you recall
How I failed you repeatedly
When I would not play ball.

LeRoy Heckman
Rockford, Illinois

Missing

Where are you, Little Girl,
   womb-remembered,
      screamed crimson into the world
         naked,
            nourished wiped
                        walked
                        tickled
                        tucked
                        jiggled
                        jellied
                        mended
                        measled
                        taped
                        tutored
                        braided
                        braced
                        partied
                        protected
                     financed
                     photographed
                   dressed
                 danced
              consoled
              and
              counselled
              by
              t
          o h
        n   e
       a   r
      w   n
       o   a
        m
Will I ever know when I am a grandmother . . . . . .

Chrisine Christian
Forest City, Iowa

Generation Gap

We walked sometimes to a place we called
the moss corner. We were doing that together
even before you were born.
Slim hickories, the showy, anxious buckeye,
and that old tree we named Crabbyapple
had capitalized on a few holes in the pines'
green umbrella. There were always jays
caviling above us and redbirds cheering
and towhees scurrying through
molding, matted leaves which had nothing to do
but lie there year after year making woods earth.
I wanted you to love nature.
I didn't know people were watching us
or that you longed to follow them.
Maybe our door splintered when you slammed it.
My ears were closed. I heard what I wanted
and saw what I wanted
and all the while Time was pouring between us
a thicker and thicker stream, running

wider and wider, and I, unawares,
kept looking across, cursing my fading vision.
    (Time, you old trickster, pouring your river
    so cunningly, quietly that I did not know,
    I am on to your ruse.)
I see you faintly now, my daughter,
a glass in your hand,
crowds clamoring for you to drink
while they prepare communal beds.
There isn't a bird or a green leaf anywhere.
I want to shout across that chasm of Time,
"Don't drink their potions
or lie down in their beds."
I want to cry, "Come, walk with me again
to the cool, green moss corner.
Hear the jay scream and the redbird cheer.
Let me adorn your hair again
with blossoms pinker than your cheeks."
Elizabeth, can you hear me calling you?

Joan Merryman Burns
Griffin, Georgia

The Lure

When I was young
I would go fishing
with Mom and Dad
   at the pond where they spent
     their honeymoon.
With each passing year
the fishing got worse,
   'til finally we caught
     none at all.
Now the folks are divorced and
I fish alone
   at the pond where they spent
     their honeymoon.
I still catch no fish,
But experience has taught me
   not to dangle the bait.

Sue Anne Briggs
North Mukegon, Michigan

The Pain

Wedded without ceremony
    she clings to you,
    faithful 'til the end.
She tosses with you in the night,
    never leaving you alone,
    like the company one keeps
        with death.
She is the first one seated
    at the holiday table
    eager to gorge herself.
On humid summer days
    she intrudes upon your Solitude
    at the shoreline.
Unable to recall
    the time before you knew her well,
    when your leadened legs
        were once feather light,
You lie in the weight
    of your own waste,
Knowing if your life should float away
    you would not swim after it.

Marilyn J. Barnes
San Jose, California

Second Place Poem

Elegy for a Marriage

Dreams fall hard.
A lifetime ago love had faith.
Time and life are alone now.
The touch . . . the closeness is gone.

What hurt?
One's best was not enough.
One yearned and prayed
But only so long can one be hurt
       . . . and rebound.
Then the hurt becomes permanent,
And love disappears.

But the desire for closeness —
The familiarity of nearness is missed —
    The emptiness of bed . . .
    The arms aching to hold . . .
    The quivering with no one to respond . . . .
        The aloneness . . .
        Such aloneness . . . .

What of the other?
    Is there no sensitivity? no regret?
        no empathy?
    Is it possible to so ignore a life
    That depended on you for nourishment?

Can one crush another
Without the greatest loss being to one's own
  self?

What of the others?
    The children, innocent and uplooking —
    Dependent on both —
    Wide-eyed at the world's beauty —
    Crying for faith and trust —
    Thrust into a void of hurt

Caused by none of their doing —
Molded into a different form —
Bent into crooked emotions —
Never to reach the best of their feeling
  potential.

What of love?
  Would you erase the glorious past of love
  To lose the anguish of the grief-full years?
  The pang is constant . . .
  The shared enrichment of tenderness and
    humanness
      remain
  But the memory of warmth makes cold
    difficult.

Melody Moody
Troy, Michigan

Marriage on the Rocks

unlike ice, rocks
    refuse to melt
and they hardly ever
    slide away
on their own . . .

but if you cut the
    roots
that hang them to
    the hillside
they know the force
    of gravity

Constance Leigh Rentel
Tacoma, Washington

Honorable Mention

Now that You are Gone

i'm so tired of remembering you
. . . of being afraid
you'll never
call again
    and being afraid
      you will

i want so much to get through
a day
without this feeling
of hope
that you might drop by
    and this feeling
      of dread
      because you might

of hope
that you might drop by
    and this feeling
       of dread
    because you might

if i see you
will i feel any worse
than i do now

if i hear your voice
will i cry again
when i hang up

no matter how many times
i tell myself
it's over with you
that we were
    beyond
      our
        limits
    as it was . . .

was it really worse than this

and did it hurt as much
to feel you fading away
while you were still here

    as it hurts

now that you are gone

Constance Leigh Rentel
Tacoma, Washington

Honorable Mention

I Never Used to Hear You

I never used to hear your voice,
When you would talk to me;
I didn't really listen;
My mind was never free.
I had so very little time,
There was so much to do;
Your voice was lost in other sounds,
That muffled what was you.

When did you come to realize
I was far too busy
To understand your needs, your dreams,
To sense Love beside me?

Today is so different;
There's little I find to do.
Stranger, even, I hear you now,
Though I've lost the sight of you.

Deloris Slesiensky
Burlington, Massachusetts

Say Again

Garbage is an endless chore —
   So is washing dishes.
Washing clothes and ironing
   Come steady as day's dawning —
And —   I'm ruddy sure
It'll all get done . . . after I'm gone.
I just wonder —
Who will be the garbage hauler —
Dish washer,
Clothes sorter,
Ironer,
Shopper,
Sweeper,
Mopper,
Taxier,
Cooker,
LOVER? kisser! hugger! WHO?

Mary Dupont
Freeport, Texas

Change

There is dew on the grass,
The kitchen faucet drips,
Coffee gurgles in the percolator.
The man sings in the shower,
The housewife waters ferns and philodendrons.
Small ripples with designs upon the sand
Tat edgings on the shore.
High on the moutain a waterfall splashes.

Rain stripes the windowpanes,
The faucet drips,
The coffee boils,
Stains pattern the ceiling
As gutters overflow,
And water from the mountain floods the valley
While angry waves crash on the shore
And dig deep furrows in the sand.

In the morning there is dew on the grass,
The faucet drips, the coffee gurgles,
But the shower is silent.
Subdued waves caress the wounded sand,
High on the mountain the waterfall splashes,
And in the kitchen
Tears drop, one by one,
Upon the table.

June L. Shipley
Highland, Indiana

That Man's Lobster

Time wave to
    tropical weekend bleary,
eyed a sand never through.

Micro-fone, herd of tiny voices wailing
Camera black — fannies flying.
Burning wide eyes, and
    pestering flies
The poor despair with
    long knotted hair.

So in dreadlock tone or
    rattled moan, he cries
"here man, only ten dollar man"
    He usually wins, and
still he starves.

Though one did not, who
    sang and moaned,
    through smokey clogged-up platinum phone.
The money pours with
        contracts flying
        while
within shack a mother lies,
her mind is dying.

Lauren McDowell-Kurszewski
Milwaukee, Wisconsin

To N.F.J.

Since you can no longer chew
they kindly grind your food for you;
father, father, all alone
the joys you knew forever gone.
Your slender hands are candle white,
your face a waxen mask, despite
the occasional smile that flickers when
we bring you news of some old friend.
Father, father, unaware
of all but this unloving care;
smile at me! Please *don't* just sit!
Delight me with your puckish wit!
(Now and then a glimmer shows
in recognition, but soon goes).
Father, father, frail and old
I'll love you till your blood runs cold
and you are rooted deep in death.
Dear old man, let go your breath!

Evelyn J. Boettcher
Rockford, Illinois

Many Things Fall

stars
kisses from lips
swollen from the love heat
seasons
slowly from view.

Big Leaf Maple
drops crisp reminders
of change
   death and change
golden hands
large as life
grip the earth
curl up into themselves
until stiff.

Outside the nursing home
timeworn bodies droop
over cradle-chairs
in the sun that plays no favorites
bleached nurses visit
double rooms rewinding
clocks to bring tomorrow
on schedule.

Maple leaves continue falling
the courtyard now a carpet
of death rattles
in the wind.

Pre-dinner spirits
are wheeled through sliding doors
several leaves are carried inside
on someone's last breath.

Mary Lou Sanelli
Sequim, Washington

Prognostication (1)

Darling, many times I've tried to quell
That sickening feeling deep inside
When I foresaw that sometime
I'd sit beneath the lilac tree
And watch the dappled shadows
Quivering with ecstacy of young
Love and tender life, shower down
Powdered-gold, green-gold
Across the velvet lawn; and
Listen for your steps and voice,
And yet be conscious that
They'd never come again!
Something akin to useless, senseless
Agony always gripped my heart
And squeezed the life blood all away
And made the universe stand still.
For a moment it always seemed so real
When I pictured how hopeless
All the world would be
If you left and never
Returned to me!

Dorothy Moore
Dowagiac, Michigan

Prognostication (2)

Now, today it is reality.
If the sun shines through the
Leaves and blooms above —
If dappled shadows shower down
Powdered-gold, lilac-gold
Across the velvet lawn,
I do not see.
Everything is swimming in a
Vague and green blurred mass edged
With gold and flanked with black,
Beyond a wall of liquid crystal
Burning! I feel the old recurring
Pain intensified because I'll listen
For your step and voice throughout
Eternity and know that I'll never see
Or hear again.

Dorothy Moore
Dowagiac Michigan

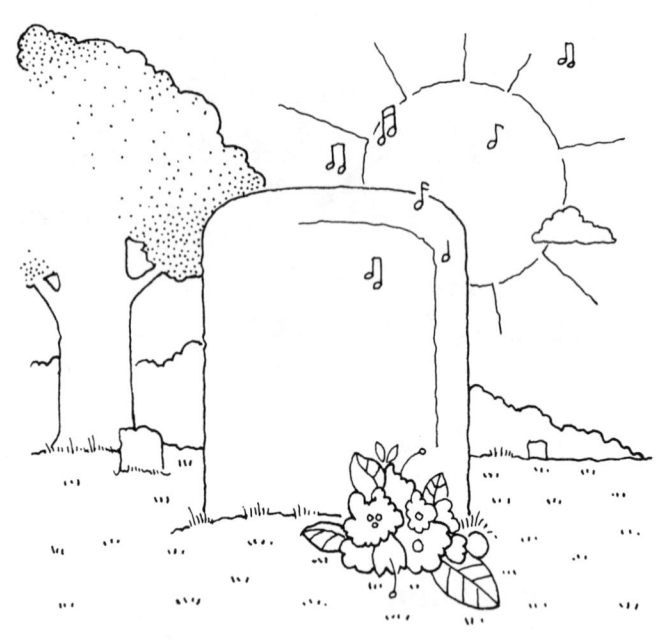

Going Home

I went to your grave
seeking you
And the winter sun shone bright
through my tears
I called your name and caressed
the cold stone they left
to mark your time in this world
And I felt you
Like a song in my head
I heard you
And I was comforted.

*T. R. Felice
Sikeston, Missouri*

Seasoned with S's

MARIANNE BERN came to this country from England in 1954 with her pianist husband. She has been writing serious as well as humorous poems for many years, both in Engish and in her native German. . . . **DONDEENA CALDWELL**, missionary-teacher in Mexico and Brazil for 18 years, now edits *Church of God Missions* magazine and is a speaker for conventions. She writes articles & for church publications, travels extensively, and spoils her 2 grandchildren. . . . **DORIS M. COLTER,** mother of 3, is a graduate of the University of Michigan. . . **EDNA (OTTO) DAME**, 76, a physical education with a B.S. from Eastern Michigan University and a P.P.E. from Eastern University in Chicago, has taught for 45 years. She enjoys handicrafts & gardening. This is her first published poem. . . . **THOMAS FOLEY**, 56, has worked the past 11 years in chemical abuse treatment with teenagers & adults. He has been writing for 15 years as a hobby. He is studying for his B.S. in psychology, specializing in chemical abuse counseling. . . . **MARTHA K. GRAHAM's** biographical sketch appears in Chapter 1. . . . **SUZANNE KELSEY**, 27, lives in the country near Iowa Falls. Mother of a boy and one child on the way, she works for a local veterinary company. . . . **JEAN KENNEDY** won first prize in the 1981 CSS Publications poetry contest; her bio appears in Chapter 3. . . .

RALPH KUDISH, a late bloomer, published his first poem in November 1981. He has completed a novel which his literary agent has high hopes of publishing. His chief hobby is music. **SISTER MONICA LAMMERS,** a retired food service supervisor, has been interested in poetry since first grade. The nature poetry she writes is inspired by memories of the homestead she grew up on in Beaher County in Minnesota. . . . **JOY (SMITH) LEISTER,** 28, has never outgrown her sensitivity to the weather. But in the past year she has discovered that close with people can be so potent that often not even a drizzly day can succeed in dampening her spirits. . . . **J. KAY LOWE**, 42, enjoys jogging, quilting & night classes. . . . **MARILYN J. ROMINE MATTIX**, 29, is a court reporter for the Fifth Judicial District of Iowa. She has written poetry for many years as a way of expressing her feelings; this is her first published poem. . . . **GARY D. MOORE** says, "I never wrote for publication until 1980. I like to write of the common but often overlooked happenings of everyday life. I currently reside in Aurora, Colorado, where I plan to continue writing." . . .

PATTI ANN NEMEC, is an avid photographer who plans to write prose & poetry to accompany her photographs. She works at the Cedar Rapids Public Library, and recently received an associate of arts degree from Kirkwood Community College by attending night classes. . . . **GRACE RASMUSSEN** says she does more talking about poetry than writing. She enjoys speaking whenenever asked, encouraging all ages to participate in the rewarding art form. . . . **RUSSELL T. RUNNELS**, 59, earned his M.S. in mining engineering from the University of Kansas in 1951 and is now director of quality control at the Monarch Cement Company. He likes reading history and archeology. This is his first attempt at publishing poetry. . . . **NANCY A. SMITH**, 39, is a wife and mother of 4 and an avid swimmer and jogger. She has a B.A. degree in romance languages and some graduate credits in English literature. She is a free-lance writer and part-time editor for Iowa State Press. . . . **SARALYN McAFEE SMITH** was born in Georgia but grew up in New Jersey. She earned her A.B. degree in history with a minor in English at Sweet Briar College in Virginia. A former English teacher, she is now a legal secretary who enjoys walking, needlepoint and cross-stitching.

Seasoned with S's

Silent shadows
Storms of sleet and snow
Stocking caps, scarves, snowshoes
Streets sprinkled with salt and sand
Skis, sleds, skates
Sub-zero Saturdays
    Surprisingly surviving

Sublime sunshine!
Stimulated senses
Slick, slippery spots
Steamy sidewalks
Sloshing shoes
Swelling streams
    Signs of spring!

Scarlet sunsets
Sunglasses, shorts, sandals
Suddenly sluggish, scorching sunlight
Searching for shade
Swimming, sunbathing, sweating
Sultry nights, shimmering stars
    Someday . . . summer

Patti A. Nemec
Cedar Rapids, Iowa

April's Spring

Raindrops
    Reflect the violet's lavender-blue!

Daffodils
    Change water puddles

Into
    Yellow butter pools!

Apple blossoms
    Float against an azure sky!

Plum trees
    Send their perfume sweet

Out
    On the soft spring breeze!

Walnut
    And mountain ash

Put forth
    Their new born leaves!

April
    Blesses the good earth

With beauties such as these.

Sister Monica Lammers
Detroit Lakes, Minnesota

Early Summer

Warm nights
the birds' songs mingle
with the voices of mothers
calling, "Come Home."

Dusk falls too fast
not even the birds
are willing to call
it quits.

Disgruntled,
the kids drag their bats
shuffling home,
not quite satisfied.

I like
sitting by my open window
knowing how they feel,
remembering.

Remembering the grin
of a wide open fly ball
finding the warm leather
of my glove.

Jean Marie Schultz
Stillwater, Minnesota

Summer Comes Again

Do not march to the common drummer;
   Listen for the flute from the mountain
   For truth comes in little whispers . . .
     from unlikely places;
Happiness is more elusive than the elves
   and does not cage well.

When happy, shout from the hilltops,
When melancholy, watch the moon
   Over darkened valleys,
Listen to the whispers from the past
   As you walk the ancient avenues
     And, in so doing
You live some each day
   Which is needed,
     For
Summer comes again, unbidden . . .
   And Autumn follows . . . too soon.

Russell T. Runnels
Humbolt, Kansas

40th Street Summer

HOT DAMN! I love summer,
crabgrass and sweat, mosquitoes and flies,
sunburn, fishin' and lies.
Swimmin' n' women and
cold chicken lunch,
little league games, and Capn' Crunch.
The rattle de rattle of electric fans,
the clinkity clink of soda pop cans.
hollyhocks and roses
and hayfever noses,
poison ivy medication
from a two week vacation.
A visit from a cousin
and bumble bees buzzin'.
Dragon fly evenings
and whippoorwill nights,
washing the car
and water fights,
bluegrass festivals
and fresh garden vegetables,
Praying for rain
and waiting for the sun,
just to play again
when work is done.
Pony kegs and pig fries,
hummingbirds and butterflies,
Just cruising the river of life,
and wishing,
summer would never end.

Gary D. Moore
Council Bluffs, Iowa

Hidden Beauty

What power of God came to lure me
To the secrets He meant to unfold?
In the deep, cool, depths of the swamplands,
I see rare lady slippers of gold.

There was no beaten path to your doorway,
As I pushed the tangled brush through,
I waded in pools and on mosses,
But was greatly rewarded by you.

I stood silent, awed by your presence,
And knew I'd greatly been blessed,
To see your delicate colors,
In nature's own verdure you're dressed.

Your presence shall be my secret;
Your beauty is mine to behold;
No one shall crush you or pick you;
You'll never be bartered or sold.

How much of life's hidden beauties
Are missed as we hurry by
On the well trodden paths and highways
Where we ne'er see the earth or the sky?

Edna Dame
Northport, Michigan

Night

I am quiet repose and dreams
Whose realm regenerates and heals,
Re-charging the body's amperes for the day,
A haven for the tired and sore.

Sometimes, I seem to have no end,
For those who silently lie and wait, devoid of sleep,
Until I leave with my unpaid claims.

I am the signal for some to work:
The watchman on his lonely rounds,
The patrolman cruising by,
The factory hand on the third shift,
The student cramming with no distractions of the day,
His desk lamp burning on and on.

I am the velvet mantle where young lovers move,
Laced with moonlight's silvery beam,
Casting its magic sheen,
Upon hair and face and wonderful vows,
And I became unforgettable.

My shroud is used, at times, for stealth,
For deeds too ugly for the garish light of day.
When my innards are lashed by flashing bullets,
And screaming sirens and red, flashing strobe lights.
Then I descend with fear.

It is thru me one sees the clearest.
Points of light so far away, in space so vast,
That make all this earth beneath, far and wide,
But a tiny space probe on God's orbit,
Housing myriad tinier atom-like motes,
That move and talk and live such important lives.

Ralph Kudish
Bolingbrook, Illinois

Rainy Day

What to do on a rainy day
      when the sky is gray
and I am blue . . .
      what to do?

The sodden world makes
      my heart forlorn,
and I sit and mourn by the window sill
      asking still

What to do on a dreary day
      with no one to play . . .
and I'm no fun,
      only one.

Grieving for joys the raindrops drown
      my tears roll down . . .
hot, salty pain
      during rain.

What to do on a soggy day
      when the sun's bright ray
is blocked from view . . .
      Oh! What to do?

Joy (Smith) Leister
Ames, Iowa

Absence of Rain

Like unto the dry cracked hands,
so the soil sifting through
seems abrasive as the sands,
a gray and lifeless hue.

Troubled eyes, pleadingly lift
their gaze slowly heavenward,
looking for a sign — a gift
where long no cloud has stirred.

Oh for just a gentle shower
to quench the thirst and urge the seed.
Minute plants, budding flower,
soft-soaking rain is all they need.

To the North grand thunderheads
hov'ring fierce and high
silent prayer upon the lips
supplication earth to sky.

Flashing fireworks light the clouds
dancing white and pink and bright
empty promises — teasing temptress
thund'ring far into the night.

Tomorrow yet another day
and with a hope it brings
life-bestowing, cleansing rain,
the benevolence of Spring.

J. Kay Lowe
Spirit Lake, Iowa

Autumn Mood

Autumn rain is falling,
Ropes of misted thread,
And the walks are covered
With a leafy spread.

Melancholy blackbirds
Flap their soggy wings,
Perching on the railing
Of deserted swings.

Storms whip trees and flowers
Into disarray.
Once again life's cycle
Moves toward decay.

Everything is mortal,
Love — a memory . . .
There will be an autumn
That I'll never see . . .

*Marianne Bern
Mount Vernon, Iowa*

Leavings

The season for leavings comes,
a gathering in, a turning in, a going in.
Corn stubble trashes the fields,
grayed in the sweeping wind.
Leaves cluster in a round dance
and, spent, rest under bushes
and crisp down to dirt.
Frost chills the still green grass
in morning premonition.

The gatherings are stored and locked;
the leavings left to blow
or raked and sacked at curbs.
Smelling smoke instead of marigolds,
bitten by wind instead of summer thorns,
I rush from doorway into doorway,
hurrying, back turned
against the wind that
is coming . . . comes . . . has come.

Jean Kennedy
Waterloo, Iowa

The Music of Autumn

Autumn: *chanson triste,*
spider-fingered notes
weaving tonal webs in filagree,
dew-studded duets.

Melancholy music
from beads of blackbirds
strung on abacus telephone wires,
cawing summer's dirge.

Melodies, mist-muffled,
of cloud-shrouded wind
softly rustling dry arpegios
on cornstalk keyboards.

Interlude at harvest,
bittersweet refrain
in counterpoint of gold over gloom
as summer sings amen.

Dondeena Caldwell
Anderson, Indiana

Alms Aims

Come some balm to heal this wound
Rain calls of the morning dove
Horizon's bright evening star
Only echo and deepen pain
Aching winters one by one
Ushering summer shadows
Bring not balm but endurance

Grace Rasmussen
Manilla, Iowa

October

October's the spriteliest girl of the year —
Her manner's refreshing and so full of cheer.
She's usually seen sporting a vivid new coat
With splashes of scarlet and gold 'round her
  throat.
A marvelous lady, she never complains;
She dances in sunlight, but also in rains.
She also loves mystery and wears a disguise,
Though she's easily unmasked by her sparkling
  eyes.
Her age is no secret — she's no tender girl;
But she's seldom inactive — her life is a whirl!
Come, dance with October and give her a try —
She'll soon steal your heart, as she's dazzled your
  eye!

Saralyn McAfee Smith
Dodge City, Kansas

Watcher in the Mountains

Days went by.
I waited to hear a tumbling
from rocky thrones of the mountains
to know for myself
how the reign of the range was ending.
    At the foot of the cliff
    was a count of rocks
    sometime fallen to history.
Dawns came and went,
nothing happened.
No wash of rain or nudge of ice
loosened a single stone
for a fated roll to the canyon.
Attacks of the seasons,
reducing me,
did not touch the mountains.

Darrell H. Bartee
Wichita, Kansas

Haiku

Bare black tree branches
are long bent fingers
beckoning us to climb the sky.

Esther Edleman
Lost Nation, Iowa

November Song

My time of year has come.
Outside, the great oaks lift their nude limbs
    against the
moon.

Outside the heavy-winged geese
Are melting down into the misty reaches of the
    marsh.

Bitter is the wind.

And a hungry fox barks among the withered
    tamarack on the ridge.

Bitter is the quiet singing of the cricket.

And the silent river lies black beneath still reeds.

Follow the trail of the wounded buck,
Over the marsh and deep into the desolate hills.

My time of the year has come.

Thomas Foley
La Crosse, Wisconsin

Sad Thoughts May Linger

Frightened by my opened door,
a score of glint-tailed grackles flee
in panic to the nearby tree
and there, like frost-struck blackened fruit,
cling lifeless, sour — silently.

    They are huddled lumps in muffled trees
    bunched against the numbing freeze
    watching stern-eyed as I go
    hunched against the blowing snow.

    Fingers of that skeletal tree
    strum out winter's threnody.
        I pause to listen
        but pause too long
        and so am caught by the siren song.

If robins blossom on that bough
and winter melts to golden spring
it just may be that I am still
beneath the black bird's wing.

Doris M. Colter
Dearborn, Michigan

Winter Storm Watch

Wind
does not know
how to stop
snow
from falling
in curtains
of cold
like sheets steeped
in springtime
gathering sun.
Twilight braids
light into sleep
across deep
drifting dunes
molding the
landscape to
hoary iced desert.
Saplings bend
like willows weeping
sorrow
to stiff tears
that reflect in
the street lights
till they too are
snuffed out
like a wick
with moist thumb
and only
whistling blackness
remains.

Nancy Smith
Ames, Iowa

Cabin Fever

This winter
This eternal, cold, damp time
Has invaded my life so long
That I can no longer discriminate
Whether the mice are in the basement
Or
Padding about in my head.
And the boxelder bugs —
Is it my imagination —
Or do they multiply before my eyes,
Lighting on all parts of me,
As if I were a chair.
The cats are even bewildered.
They've stopped sniffing for
spring
When I open the door.

*Suzanne Kelsey
Iowa Falls, Iowa*

Winter Night

Outside the rime-cold panes
the winter night
prints deep blue shadows
over white.

Against the bitter north
trees crook their backs
and lean bare branches over
patterned tracks.

Cedars hush the chickadees'
fluttering sound,
stir and sigh and shiver snow
to the ground.

Warm and lax in your fur,
fox, lie low.
Hawk, sweep your dark shadow
over other snow.

Small prey, wherever you are,
no sound, no smallest tune.
Continue, owl, deep in the woods,
to question the moon.

Martha K. Graham
Macomb, Illinois

Honorable Mention

Winter's End

Even I, who crave the Spring, cannot but stand
in awe of Winter's strength and beauty when
evergreen boughs hang low in silent resignation
and wanton Winter once again defies the onward
march of time and muffles the cry of Spring
beneath a blanket of snow.

It's as if she fears we'll soon forget her
crystal designs that glisten on an otherwise
barren tree or the virginal snow which brings
such peace as it softly envelopes the starkness
left behind by Fall's fading colors
And wishes to etch upon our minds one final
testimony of her worth so we might reflect
on and long for her return when Summer's
swelter stifles.

Marilyn J. Romine Mattix
Des Moines, Iowa

Interpreters
(What the Dream Is Saying)

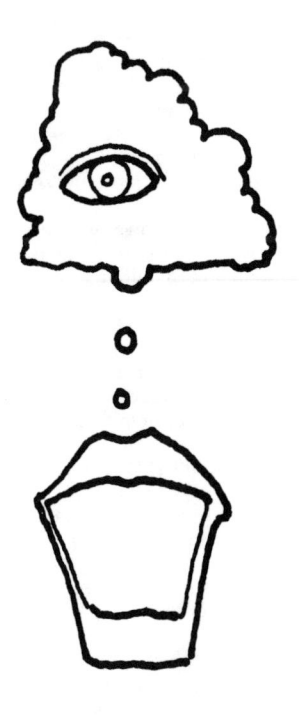

Interpreters

CHARLOTTE H. BRUNER is professor of French and coordinator of "Third-World Cultures." She has published critical articles and translations of francophone poets of Africa and the Caribbean. Since 1974, she and her husband, David, have produced three series of half-hour radio programs —consisting of interviews, readings, and commentary — concerning contem— porary Third World writers. Over one hundred programs to date have been broadcast over WOI-Radio.

DAVID K. BRUNER, professor of English at Iowa State University, was born in 1912 in St. Louis, Missouri. He received A.B. and M.A. degrees from Washington University and a Ph.D from the University of Illinois. He has been teaching writing and comparative literature for many years and most recently has been presenting literary readings and commentaries over WOI-Radio.

DENNIS BROWN was an instructor of English for six years at Ellsworth Community College before embarking on a new career in sales and marketing. Presently he is Director of National Accounts Sales for Chicago with Ryder Truck Lines, Inc., and teaches part-time at Moraine Valley College.

DAN McGUINESS lives in Iowa Falls, Iowa, where he teaches English at Ellsworth Community College. He also directs the Ellsworth Poetry Project, a series of readings and workshops on the campus.

MARION GREMMELS, like many women of her generation, has richocheted from teaching kindergarten, to working in libraries, to homemaking and mothering, to free-lance writing, to teaching at Wartburg College in Waverly, Iowa. She is still married to her first husband, still mothered to her two children. She received her master's degree in English from the University of Northern Iowa in 1975. She teaches Children's Literature, Creative Writing, Composition and Women and Literature at Wartburg.

BETTY HALL is a writer living near Vancouver, Washington, who has been writing more prose than poetry in the last year or so while working on her liberal arts degree at Marylhurst College in Oregon. Her poems have been published in various magazines and newspapers, and some have received awards in Oregon and Washington contests.

WILL C. JUMPER, a professor of English at Iowa State University in Ames, did his undergraduate study in chemistry at the University of California in Berkeley. While teaching in high school at Modesto, California, he earned his M.A. in creative writing and his Ph.D in American literature at Stanford. He has published short stories, poems and critical essays widely and has one book of poetry, *From Time Remembered*, 1977.

Continued on page 217...

Thirty Billion Stars

*Translation of "Trente milliards d'etoiles"
by Anthony Phelps, from Mon pays que voici,
Paris: Oswald, 1968, p. 42.*

I put the Milky Way on sale
For just a little love,
But found no bidder.

Nobody in the world
Wants to take on
Some thirty billion stars.

Nobody.

So could it be that Love
Is outworn currency
For all the human race?

Who knows?

For Those I Love

*Translation of "Pour ceux que j'aime"
by Anthony Phelps, from Mon Pays Que Voice
Paris: Oswald, 1968, p. 43*

Within my cell
For just a flower alone
I'd give a verse —
A poem entire
For just a bird,
And for the voice of one I love
I'd give a gift of prosody.

*Translated by Charlotte H. Bruner
Ames, Iowa*

The Wait

Translation of "Attente" by Anthony Phelps
Motifs pour le temps saisonnier, *Paris: Oswald, 1976. p. 52*

In my own life, confined
Between parentheses
Where laughter never passes by,
Dreaming with open eyes,

I play at Come-and Go,
Between the here — and now —
And a There problematical,
Changing my exile's periods
To curves
Of blister hollowness.

Tell me, whoever can decipher
Slow trails of snails
Tell me
Will the poet's head
Bent over fountain water
Remain forever fixed
Wed to his thirst?

Translated by Charlotte H. Bruner
Ames, Iowa

Getting Next to Me

It's an effort to throw you away,
old shirt. These scissors point out
good parts for rags. You didn't fail
where I thought you might when I
found you, slightly imperfect, marked down.
That machine-made scar is strong,
and the place I mended where barbed wire
got both of us. Actually, the elbows
went first. Then we worked in the yard
where slow abrasion by muscle and bone
wore out your back. You have a back
and arms and a neck, and deserve better
than being cut to rags — you deserve
a funeral pyre made with yard trimmings.
You'll rise whole and slightly imperfect
in my mind, old shirt — marked down
as less than skin, more than cloth.

Rites

Hollyhocks never made it to our table.
I remember dandelions in a water glass,
and violets. Roses always got a vase.

Sometime in summer hollyhocks would bloom
in the background, lounging against a fence
by the alley. Bees were invited to that table.
Just once I closed a flower around a bumblebee
then stood there worrying how to let go.

When I smell flowers for all occasions
I want to be among the uninvited. Yet I stand
alongside forced blooms tied with ribbons,
listen to the buzz, and wonder how to let go.

Betty Hall
Vancouver, Washington

Born Losers

Every key in this box
knew its way around
a lock on something valued.
Yet the value of a key
and its lock keeps them
mostly apart. If I'd tagged
all these keys, I'd know
which keys remain
part of a team.
Locked or unlocked,
some things wear out.
Others are lost, or lose
their value — and the keys,
though good, are doomed.
That roundheaded key
looks like Charlie Brown.
Lined up, my keys
are the whole
comic strip.

Betty Hall
Vancouver, Washington

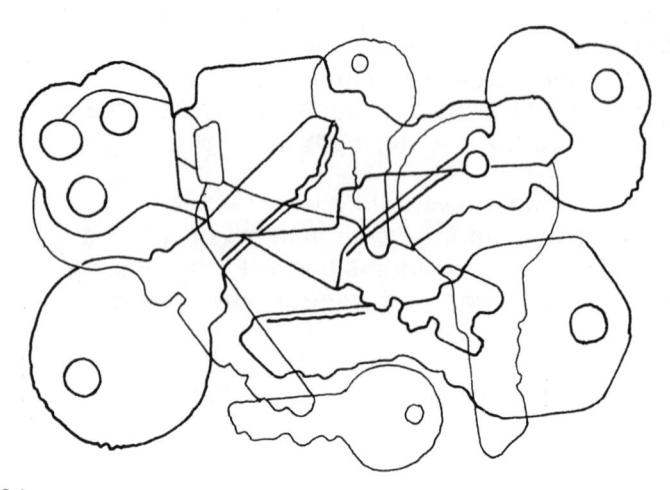

Advice to a Collector

Pinion its pattern neatly
on velvet-covered cork.
Carefully pierce its head
with the poignant, nerveless pin.

Stifle the twinge of anguish
that shakes reluctant fingers.
Beaten against tomorrow,
the fragile wings would shatter.

Keep, under glass, its mummy.
Like opal-dusted moths,
dreams have fulfilled their purpose
by merely being born.

Advice to a Builder

Spread yielding mortar evenly
between the chunks of stone.
This wall you build must stand against
assault of blood and bone.

Weighing each fragment carefully,
note its especial form;
for each was blasted out of self,
pulsating, soft, and warm.

The climate of adversity
solidifies to rock
what once was only yielding stuff
unused to cold and shock.

This ruthless wall will serve you well,
no spot built weak or thin,
to hold the screaming forces out —
and lock the torrent in.

Will C. Jumper
Ames, Iowa

Valentine

In tin cups
the heart is carried.
Red-suited,
we clang them like bells
for a holiday.

Gentle beggar,
the heart is a cupful of silk,
hardly enough to wear,
still,
we rally our flags
a taste for the addict
a tongue on threads
tight and shiny.

Our bones are surprised
at this coupling
the attempted lock
of hips
and hearts
the exhaustable prayer
repeated

It is a small wound,
the hole in the heart,
pricked from the inside out,
spilled into cups
and bells, and banners

There is a sorrow in its emptying
that is neither deadly
or accidental.

Kathleen Peirce
Davenport, Iowa

Fog

The city is delirious
with hiding.

Trees
shrug off
their show of sensibilities.
Look how the limbs rest
nearer the trunk,
like the altar boy's plate,
tired of grace
and offerings.

The railroad is shy.
The river is primping its banks.
Fish have mistaken the air
for the sea —
they are leaping up
with open mouths.
They have taken traffic
with sky.

Streetlamps release
the bondage of poles.
They are fickle as
matchlight
and cannot stand still
in their darkness.

Only the dogs
are dogs tonight,
meeting on lawns
their paws to the ground
noses in the air
wetting their whiskers
on fish.

Kathleen Peirce
Davenport, Iowa

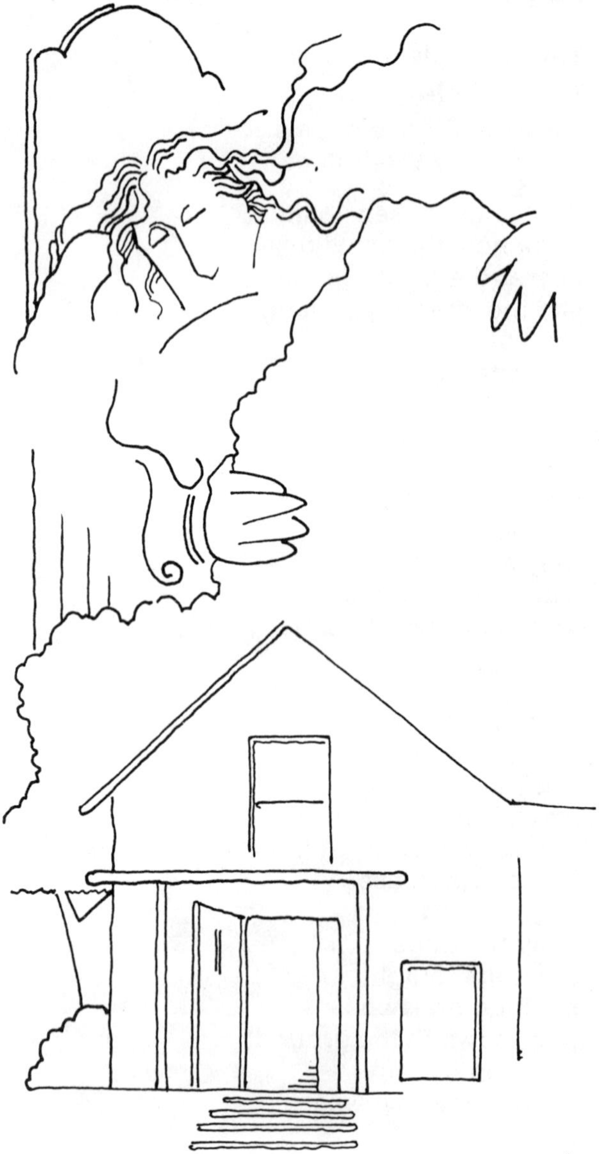

What the Dream Is Saying

The house you are dreaming is empty
except for your father
weeping into his poems
except for your mother in skirts
dipping the font the holy water

Lie down in every room.
The floorboards become you,
flat-eyed and brown as your hair.

Stand still in your sister's closet.
Run your hand through the harp of her dresses.
Her name is being played in silk.

Fold yourself now
as a sweater an envelope
and wait in the bureau drawer.

When your grandfather dies
take his bed as your own.
Lie down in the palm of his mattress
and think of his face.

You have come back again.
You are tired of returning.
The walls remember you laughing,
your body's deceit as it changed,
grew hair,

and the first time you painted your face.
The house remembered all this.
It remains sturdy despite you.

This dream is almost over.
When you wake
let your eyes run the length of your bones,
and think about where you are living

Kathleen Peirce
Davenport, Iowa

Charlie
(Charles H. Carrico, M. F. H., 1882-1966)

We hunt tomorrow at nine.
I never sleep the night before.
I cannot when I think of skimming through timber,
across fields, watching for holes,
alert for the one fence my gray always tries to
 duck.
And Charlie will know, he'll know.
He doesn't need to see.
With ears like a woods creature
whose life depends upon it,
he knows every horse behind him
and when he detects uninterrrupted pace
he'll know we didn't jump.
And how can I sleep when I hear the squeak of
 leather,
when I feel the gray's thin skin,
the softness of the creamy French silk
wrapped around my neck,
and the mud from the horse in front of me
flying up at me —
what a glorious cleanup it will be.
There's no sleep when I know
we'll gather later to talk it over,
warming ourselves with cocoa or coffee,
brandy or port,
and Charlie's presence.
And that as we honor our Master,
consummate hunter and sportsman,
he in turn will praise his hounds,
whom he has trained
only to chase,
to track down,
but never to kill.

Sarah P. Simmons
Cedar Rapids, Iowa

Conversation

Most New York cabbies used to talk.
They had a reputation to live up to —
their opinions were legends.
But after awhile taking on passengers became
    dangerous
and a heavy window closed off philosophy.

Once, rolling along, block after block,
he asked perfunctory questions
but in a perfectly interested way,
so I responded in earnest.
That over, he took his wider stance.
I liked him. I listened.
And I believed when he explained,
"This here ain't my real life yet."
I saw part of my face in his mirror
and promised myself,
"Nor is this mine."

Sometimes still I wonder about that cabbie
and if anything changed.
Or does he still believe
as he counts the miles,
the years,
and waits
and waits
and waits . . .

Sarah P. Simmons
Cedar Rapids, Iowa

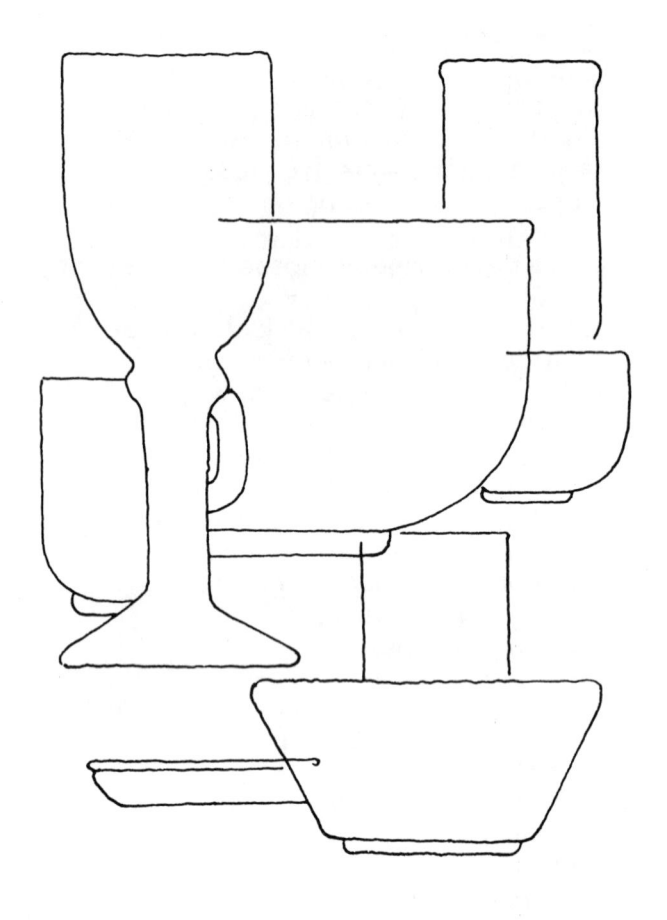

At the Potter's House

That summer day —
we went to look at pots
in a farmhouse on a hill.
We sat at a table, set just for us,
showing the pieces to best advantage.
The brown plates, cups, saucers, and wine glasses
were admirable.

Nothing was on the plates
nor in the cups or glasses.
The house was so cool, made up, attractive but
empty as the cups in front of us.
I shivered.
My mind and gaze wandered out of the windows,
so I followed them.
I stood under an elm tree,
listening to the softness of the leaves.
When the sun struck just so,
the leaves became the same
lime color
as my green and white dress.

The wind surged under my skirt, making it billow
so that I looked as round and well formed
as the huge planter spilling ivy from the porch roof.
I felt unaccountably beautiful.
Loving my new pear shape, the tree, the sun, the wind,
I wished more days could be like that one,
there where I stood,
and in a farmhouse I would warm
by filling the plates, the glasses,
and placing colorful napkins beside them.

I leaned against the tree,
absorbing the sun,
wishing the fullness were true
and that a child was gathering
with the wind
under my white
and lime green dress.

Sarah P. Simmons
Cedar Rapids, Iowa

The Day Is June

When the heavens storm and thunder
O'er a world of rape and plunder,
Have you ever stopped to wonder
Why we sing this mortal tune?
Soughts by pests and politicians,
Snide complaints and worse petitions,
Driven by our superstitions
Somewhere fast and nowhere soon,
Have you questioned constant coping,
Marred and starred by human hoping?
Have you wearied of the groping?
Come with me; the day is June.

    Leave your office and your sorrow;
    Both will wait until tomorrow;
    Time is something you can't borrow.
    Come with me; the day is June.
    Leave your greasy gears and gaskets,
    Looming ledgers, laundry baskets.
    Leave your coffins and your caskets.
    Come with me; the day is June.

Come to where the water merges
With the sand, its languid surges
Singing songs of secret urges,
Whispered songs of love in June.
Come to where the air is truer
Just because the water's bluer;
Come to where your cares are fewer
Just because the day is June.
June abhors the rank pedantic;
June delights in sights romantic;
June invites the childish antic.
Come with me; the day is June.

    Buoyed by dreams and wafting breezes,
    Watch the cloud that plays and teases

*With the sun until it eases
Gently past to parts unknown.
Feel the sun, supreme and doting,
In the flush of love, devoting,
Send erotic embers floating
To and through each wintered bone.*

Watch the winsome playmates thrashing
Through the water, gaily splashing
Cares away, their whimsies dashing
Ever forward, ever grand.
Watch the tan tomorrows fetching
Simple spheres, their muscles stretching
Toward the sun, their movements etching
Careless patterns in the sand.
Watch the distant couple learning
Love's eternal, living burning;
Feel the warmth of youthful yearning,
Walking wonders, hand in hand.

*Watch the child of six uncover
Shells and rocks as playmates hover
Round about till all discover
Priceless treasures in the sand.
Watch the child of sixty wading
Just beyond the near-by shading,
Finding, free from time or fading,
Priceless pleasures in the sand.*

June is Nature's grand endeavor
To disprove the blight of Never;
Nothing can be wrong forever —
Not when God is in His June.
June is Nature's perfect passion
Spread about in equal ration;
Nothing fails in worth or fashion —
Not when God is in His June.
June abhors the rank pedantic;
June delights in sights romantic;

June invites the childish antic.
Come with me; the day is June.

Leave your tilling and your tractors;
Leave your files of facts and factors;
Leave your fare of re-run actors;
Come and walk upon the dune.
Leave your office and your sorrow;
Both will wait until tomorrow;
Time is something you can't borrow.
Come with me; the day is June.

Curt L. Sytsma
Des Moines, Iowa

Interpreters
Continued from page 200...

DONALD S. PADY, a native of Kansas City, Missouri, is a reference librarian at Iowa State University. Since 1973 he has edited *Annual Bibliography of Midwestern Literature in Mid-America*.

KATHLEEN PEIRCE lives in Davenport, Iowa, where she is a student and teacher of poetry. Her work has been published in the United States and Great Britain. Ms. Peirce gives readings of her work often, most recently at the Oxbow School of Art in Saugatuck, Michigan.

SARAH P. SIMMONS, ex-New Yorker, writing since age four, began poetry study in 1972 at the University of Iowa, where she matriculates. Published in Virgina, Illinois, Iowa and California, she received Honorable Mentions in all prior CSS Publications poetry anthologies and a Third Prize. She works on her first book of poems. Her life strongly influenced by Kazantzakis' and William Stafford's writings, she has studied with Stafford.

CURT L. SYTSMA, a Des Moines attorney, is a nationally syndicated columnist who comments in verse on social and political issues. The author of the recently released book published by CSS Publications, *The Rhyme & Reason of Curt Sytsma*, he is presently at work on a novel.

Concentric Circles
Continued from page 138...

exchange student came back for Christmas.... **SANDY LISKA**, 39, has been writing poetry for 3 years. Her work has appeared in numerous anthologies throughout the U.S. She is a believer in the eternal validity of the human soul —a free bird in the truest sense.... **NELLE McCAIN** started writing poetry in high school and is still writing at the age of 92. She has had many poems published in local newspapers & magazines.... **LAUREN McDOWELL-KURSZEWSKI**, 23, previously an art major, is now studying poetry & writing at the University of Wisconsin, Milwaukee, thanks to Christine Ranschau and James Liddy.... **SALLY C. MEDERNACH**, 50, has shared her verses with family & friends since age 10. Recently returning to college to study art, she is creating a folio of original, embossed-serigraph prints of images with verse. She is planning a printmaking workshop for a sixth grade creative writing class.... **BECKY FOGHT MELBY**, 29, is a homemaker who enjoys camping, writing & trying to keep up with her 3 sons.... **MELODY MOODY** is a pseudonym for a divorced, retired schoolteacher who is also the mother of 3. After retiring, she found time to pursue her first love — writing - and has had several published; she also helps edit a "little" magazine.... **BETTY C. MOORE**, experienced wife, mother, homemaker, desires — at age 60 — to shift gears to inspiring poet. She loves nature, particularly mushrooms, wildflowers and birds.... **DOROTHY MOORE** is an English major & special art graduate of Ball State University and has been writing poetry since age 14. She is stepmother to 8, step-grandmother to 25, and step-great-grandmother to 3. A retired teacher, she cooks, sews, paints & reads....

KAREN ANN MURGUIA, 28, mother of 2, has been published twice previously. "I run a small domestic services agency and have been writing since high school. My poems, mostly inspired by family, are composed in odd snatches of time, jotted down on paper bags or scraps of paper."... **KATHY A. OLSON**, 29, feels good fortune in having had the opportunity to grow up and still reside in the Coon Valley-LaCrosse, Wisconsin, area. She writes for peace of mind, attributing her stimulus to the people & scenery of the region.... **CONSTANCE LEIGH RENTEL's** bio appears in Chapter 7.... **WILLIAM P. RIDDLE**, 30, from rural Colfax, Iowa, has been included in all 5 CSS Publications anthologies. He has been enjoying several months of being "gainfully unemployed," but is hoping to find a job soon. He enjoys gardening, fishing, photography & poetry....**DeANN RICHTSMEIER**, 18, is a radio/T.V. broadcasting major at Brown Institute in Minneapolis, Minnesota. She has been writing for 4 years; this is her first published work.... **DOROTHY M. ROSS**, a legal secretary, has been married 28 years and is the mother of 3. She has been writing poetry since one-room grade school days, and her poems have appeared in many publications. Active in DAR, she is working on her fifth novel, set in contemporary Lincoln Land historically rich Illinois clime; she also writes free-lance short articles.... **MARY LOU SANELLI**, 25, has been published widely in poetry anthologies & magazines. She is involved in public radio readings & private ones as well. She has recently had her first compiled collection, *The Wandering Portrait*, published....**DELORIS SELINSKY** is a program analyst working with the U.S. Army. She has been writing poetry for publication for a year and a half and has managed to get a few of the poems published.... **JUNE SHIPLEY** has a lively interest in, and concern for, people, animals & nature. She also enjoys history, art & cooking. She has had several poems published and has won awards locally and nationally.... **JUDY WHITE** is a teacher, professional musician, mother of 2 sons and wife of a Presbyterian minister. She enjoys needlework, crocheting and gourmet cooking....

About the Publisher

CSS Publications was conceived and founded by C. Sherman Severin and Rebecca S. Bell in 1977. It was dedicated at birth to the vitality of the small press movement.

Through the publication of five annual poetry anthologies and the highly acclaimed hardcover book, *The Rhyme & Reason of Curt Sytsma*, CSS Publications has acquired a national reputation as a respected publisher of poetry.

In its unique system, CSS Publications sponsors annual poetry contests based on the theme of "human emotions." The contest is open to individuals of all ages and from every state in the nation.

Poems entered in the contest are evaluated by a panel consisting of poets and English professors. Through a two-step procedure, judges select poems to be included in the current book and determine the prize-winning entries. The top three poems earn cash awards, and several other poems receive honorable mention. Published poets are given a complimentary copy of the book and their hometown newspapers are informed of their publication.

All poets who enter the contests are invited to the annual Poetry Day & Awards Banquet. Master of ceremonies for the event is Curt L. Sytsma, the Des Moines attorney whose poetry appears in syndication in newspapers across the country. The 1982 Banquet is scheduled to be held in Iowa Falls on November 13.

For additional information about CSS Publications, write to:

    CSS Publications
    P.O. Box 23
    Iowa Falls, Iowa 50126

Also Published by CSS Publications:

The Rhyme & Reason of Curt Sytsma (1982)

Images of Our Lives (1981)

Moments in Time (1980)

Feelings (1979)

Emotions, Emotions (1978)

CSS Publications
Post Office Box 23
Iowa Falls, Iowa 50126